UNIVERSALIS

UNIVI

D0861400

The game where every

The game where players can create
and populate the world as they desire—as they play

The game where everything that happens,
happens because a player wanted it to happen

The game where suspense comes
from the actions of other players, not from a random roll

The game whose plot evolves as you play
with no random tables, rail-roading, or scenario books

The game which requires absolutely no set up or preparation time

The game where it doesn't matter
if all of the players show up on time or at all

Begin play with only sheets of blank paper, pencils,
ten-sided dice, tokens, and plenty of imagination

ALL THE RULES YOU NEED CAN BE FOUND WITHIN THESE PAGES

TABLE OF CONTENTS

ACKNOWLEDGEMENTS & CREDITS

Ralph Mazza & Mike Holmes

PUBLISHED BY
Ramshead Publishing
Copyright Ralph Mazza 2001, 2002, 2006

INTERIOR ART
David Hedgecock
The Rabbithole@cox.net

GRAPHIC DESIGN & LAYOUT
Matt Snyder
matt@chimera.info

COVER IMAGE
Jari Tuovinen
www.arkkikivi.net

EDITORS
Andrew Morris
Ben Pope
Ruth Shaffer

ISBN-10: **0-9765126-0-2**
ISBN-13: **978-0-9765126-0-8**

UNIVERSALIS WEBSITE
www.ramshead.indie-rpgs.com

FOREWARD TO THE THIRD PRINTING

Wow, what a great ride it has been. It was early August 2002 when Mike and I picked up our first *Universalis* run from the printers on the way to our debut GenCon. We'd been working on this game for over a year, and it had transformed into something neither of us could have predicted. One by one all of the traditional trappings of role-playing games were eliminated. First to fall was the preplanned scenario, then the Game Master, and finally even traditional Player Characters. It had become a game unique in existence at that time. It was a game so different from any RPG that had come before that we wondered if anyone besides us would even want to play it. Yet play it they did, snapping up that first print run in barely four months.

In January of 2003 I bought out Mike's share of the game and financed the second print run completely out of profits from the first. I printed enough copies to last for several years; or so I thought. Now, I stand on the threshold of a third printing, again financed exclusively from sale profits. It's been an amazing three years, and since that first GenCon, I find that I have many more people to whom I owe debt of gratitude.

First, to all of the fans who purchased the game, thank you. Special thanks to those who introduced others to the game, who've played it repeatedly with different groups and even demoed it at conventions. Without your enthusiastic support, actual play, and many contributions, *Universalis* would have long since been forgotten.

I want to specifically mention Lael Buchanan, J.B. Bell, Ron Edwards, Jonathan Walton, Christopher Bradley, and Matthijs Holter. Each of you have written reviews for the game and through your impassioned depiction introduced *Universalis* to many new fans. Special thanks here go to RPG Net (**www.rpg.net**) and The Forge (**www.indie-rpgs.com**) for providing fantastic venues for small-press publishers to reach a dynamic and enthusiastic base of role-players who are eager to try something different.

Next, I want to acknowledge Jason Valore of Key 20 (**www. key20.com**). Jason has assembled an amazing catalog of games that he reps to major distributors, direct to retailers, and at a number of conventions throughout the year. It is because of Key 20 that *Universalis* is available through all of the major distributors right to your friendly local game store (and if your local game store owner doesn't carry *Universalis*, please direct them to Key 20 where they can pick up an outstanding selection of great games). I'm very proud to have created one of the first products they carried.

Thanks also to all of the contributors to the *Universalis* discussion forums at the Forge. It's quite a thrill to have fans answering questions about the game as well or better than I could. As a player of *Universalis*, you'll be sure to find answers to all of your questions there (www.indie-rpgs.com).

I want to specifically mention Roy Penrod, Christopher Bradley, Clinton Nixon, Kirt Dankmyer, Bob McNamee, Tony Irwin, Arturo González-Escribano, and Jonathan Nichol whose thoughts and contributions to the game have made it into the game as side bars throughout the text

Special thanks are owed to Mike Holmes. Even though he's not officially part of Ramshead publishing, he's been there on the forums and at the Forge booth at GenCon since the beginning. He's been a huge advocate for the game which, of course, could not have been created without him.

Thanks also to Andrew Morris, Ben Pope, and Ruth Shaffer who edited the text. Because of them it's in far better shape than it would have been.

I want to specifically acknowledge Matt Snyder, who did the layout for the original printing and has graciously handled this one as well. Matt has his own growing collection of great games, including the award-winning Dust Devils and Nine Worlds available at *www.chimera.info*.

CHANGES TO THE THIRD PRINTING

With this print run I've had the chance to make some changes to the basic text. Numerous typos and related errors have been cleaned up, of course, but more importantly, with the benefit of three years of experience and player feedback, some key sections of text have been completely rewritten for better clarity.

I've also included some additional content. *Universalis* introduced the concept of the Rules Gimmick, a formal process for introducing house rules into your game to customize your own play experience. Some of the Gimmicks that have been introduced by fans have become so widespread and commonly used that they are practically standard at this point, so I've inserted them as options in the appropriate chapters.

The rule for what happens with a tied roll in a Complication has been simplified, the Complications chapter has been rewritten with better explanations, and Chapter 1 contains a more complete description of game play designed to ease new players into the game.

While the rules have not changed significantly, there are enough changes to the text to warrant calling this the Revised edition. If you already own one of the earlier printings I think you'll be pleased to add this version to your game collection as well, especially if you had some difficulty with the early presentation. If you are reading *Universalis* for the first time, you can thank the current fans of the game for making this version much more accessible to new players.

Finally, I dedicate this book to Ruth,
without whom life would be a whole lot more empty.

CHAPTER 1:
THE BASIC CONCEPT

GETTING STARTED

Universalis is a game about creating stories. Every story needs a setting, characters, props, and a plot. You'll be developing these as you play by spending Coins. Coins are the resource that give you control over the story, and every player will have a supply of them called their Wealth. Every character you create and everything you have those characters do will cost Coins. The Coins are a way of regulating how much of the story any one person can tell at a time. Basically, every statement you make that establishes some fact about the story will cost 1 Coin.

When you run low on Coins you're actually running low on the ability to influence the story, at least until you acquire more Coins. Everyone will get a few additional Coins periodically during the game, but the best way to replenish a low supply is to introduce plot conflicts, obstacles, and Complications (often during another player's turn).

When you first sit down to play, you and your fellow players will have to decide what kind of story you're going to be telling. Is it going to be an action adventure, a romance, a mystery, or a psychological thriller? Is the mood going to be dark and gritty, a light comedy, or outrageously absurd humor? What's the setting? Is it going to be science fiction featuring space ships? Will it be set on an alien planet, or is it a future version of earth? Is it going to be fantasy, based in actual history, or a western? How strictly are you expecting the other players to abide by the conventions of the genre you're playing in? Think of your favorite books, movies, and TV shows for inspiration.

To answer these questions you'll take turns going around the table, with each player spending 1 Coin to add one element about the type of story you're going to tell (these are called Tenets in the game). For your first game, Tenets should be kept fairly basic and will often be based on cliché and familiar genre tropes. You'll keep going until everyone gets a sense about what sort of story you'll be telling. It's important not to get so involved in adding Tenets that you actually begin to tell the story itself. When someone gets a great idea for a strong opening scene you'll stop adding Tenets and begin actual play.

At this point you'll begin creating the plot of your story. The whole game is played in scenes, just like the scenes of a movie or TV show. All scenes in the game start by being framed, which just means establishing what's initially going on (who, where, and when) so the other players can visualize what's happening. The player who frames a scene will have a great deal of influence over the direction the story takes, so at the beginning of each scene everyone will have the chance to secretly bid Coins for the privilege. If you have a really great idea for what to do with the next scene, bid a lot of Coins. If you don't, bid few or none. Bids will be revealed simultaneously and whoever wins will frame the next scene and spend their bid Coins. Other bidders will get to take their Coins back.

The winner's job as scene framer is to set the stage for the rest of the players. They need to describe where the action is taking place, when it's taking place, and who's there. Once that's done, play will continue around the table with each player having the opportunity to add to the story. As players talk, one player (called the Recorder) is designated to write down, in bullet-point fashion, the important things that are said.

Everything you narrate about the story will be either Color or Fact. Color includes all of the extraneous details that make descriptions interesting and exciting but aren't really all that crucial to remember. Facts are the important elements of the story. If you think something you've said is worth writing down so others will remember it, if you want it to be an important element to the story that other players will abide by and incorporate into what they narrate, it's a Fact and needs to be paid for. If not, if it's just an entertaining tidbit that won't likely need to be referred to again, its Color and is free. Every Fact costs 1 Coin, and once you spend a Coin on something it becomes Fact. If you don't spend a Coin on it, its only Color.

Facts are important when there is a disagreement among players about a statement someone makes. Any element someone narrates about anything related to the story is subject to being challenged by one of the other players who doesn't like it or thinks they have a better idea. But once something is established as Fact it's more difficult to Challenge it later. When a disagreement arises, you discuss what you don't like and offer sugges-

8

art © 2002. david hedgecock

tions. If you can come to an agreement, great, play goes on. If you can't agree, then a full Challenge occurs where everybody bids Coins to vote for the outcome they prefer.

Some Facts will establish Components in the game. Components are people, places, and things. They are the nouns of the game. Some Facts will establish Traits that are attached to Components. Traits describe the features of and relationships between Components. They are the adjectives of the game. Some Facts will establish Events which involve Components doing things. They are the verbs and adverbs of the game. Some Facts will establish new Tenets in the game. They are the rules for the game world itself. Any noun, adjective, verb or adverb left as Color and not paid for, however, does not establish any of these things and are completely temporary and not written down.

Every Component that is currently present in a scene will belong (temporarily) to an individual player, and the player will play that Component. This includes not only characters in the story but also buildings, possessions, entire organizations, or even abstract concepts like an ideology. The player is said to Control that Component. Control will change hands frequently during play so that any player may wind up playing any Component and no Component is the sole exclusive property of any one player.

During play, players can only establish Facts relating to Components they Control. If you try to establish a Fact about a Component you don't Control you must either first Take Control of that Component or Originate a Complicationh. During Complications, players will use established Traits or spend Coins to establish new ones to add ten-sided dice to a Dice Pool. Any

9

FACTS AND COLOR

Facts: anything worth writing down so it can be remembered and enforced in play

- Tenets: Rules of the game and game setting
- Components: people places and things in the setting (nouns)
- Traits: features and relationships of Components (adjectives)
- Events: Components doing things (verbs and adverbs)

Color: any of the above that makes the description more interesting but isn't worth writing down

Trait or other Fact that can be interpreted as an advantage for the Component the player Controls will earn dice, and each player will build their own Pool of dice accordingly. These dice will be rolled to generate bonus Coins and determine the order in which the players will get to use those Coins to describe the outcome of the Complication. Manufacturing situations that put Components Controlled by different players into conflict is a key driving force of play and an important means of acquiring additional Coins

Play continues until the players agree that the story has come to an end (possibly taking multiple play sessions). Early play can appear rather chaotic as players introduce lots of characters and ideas and create many divergent plot lines. Eventually, in a flash of inspiration, one or more of the players will see a way to tie all of the many threads together into a coherent whole and begin to maneuver the game towards a climax. Often, multiple players will have different visions of what that climax should be or how it should end up. This will be when Complications start getting very large and involve lots of dice as you compete for the privilege of driving towards your preferred resolution. A finished game may be left as a complete project on its own, or you may revisit that same setting with new tales to tell. Future games may gradually build up an entire world or cycle of stories, which reuse existing Components from previous games.

That's the core of how Universalis is played. The rest of these rules will elaborate on the concepts outlined above, cover a variety of contingencies that may come up during a game, provide more specific examples, and introduce a few advanced ideas.

CHAPTER 1: THE BASIC CONCEPT

SETTING UP THE GAME

Universalis requires no pre-game preparation. To play, you'll need:

1. A supply of tokens to serve as Coins. Glass stones, beads, poker chips, or actual pocket change can all serve. 50 Coins times the number of players is a good amount for most play.

2. Blank paper and pencils. Any paper will suffice: ruled, un-ruled, a notepad, a composition book, or index cards; even sticky notes will do in a pinch.

3. A large supply of ten-sided dice (d10s). Ten per player is a good starting amount. If ten-sided dice aren't available, page 105 provides optional rules for using standard six-sided dice (d6s) instead.

4. Space to serve as the Bank, where the central reserve of Coins will be kept. Not required, but often helpful, is a set of bowls or other containers to hold the Coins and dice, especially if not playing around a table.

5. Sufficient space for each player to roll large handfuls of dice.

DESIGN NOTE

The Coin mechanic sets up a miniature economy in the game, which functions regardless of the number of Coins involved. However, different amounts of Coins will result in a different feel to play (a Coin-rich vs. a Coin-poor environment), and players are encouraged to experiment until finding the level they find most enjoyable.

In general, a game with high initial Coins will allow players to spend many Coins building the environment in the first scene before getting to the action. A game with fewer initial Coins will require getting to the action earlier because only by starting new scenes and Originating Complications can more Coins be acquired.

Each player will have a supply of Coins of their own, called their Wealth, taken from the Bank. It is suggested that you start with 25 Coins each until you become familiar with the rules. After a few sessions, you can adjust this amount to find a level that suits your style of play. The number of Coins to be used

(11)

must be chosen before selecting any Tenets.

Coins measure story power. If you spend Coins, you gain power over the story. It's that simple. A player's Wealth is a reserve of potential, but as yet unused, story power. As Coins are spent to gain immediate control over an aspect of the game, the player is simultaneously giving up some potential for control in the future. This dynamic, and the need to replace spent Coins, is what drives the game forward.

Establish one player as the group Recorder, typi-

RULES GIMMICK: RECORDER VARIANTS

Instead of nominating a single recorder you can have the person to the right of the speaking player be the recorder so the responsibility passes around the table. Or each player can keep their own record of what they say on their turns.

Instead of using regular paper, each individual Component can be recorded on a seperate index card listing its own Traits. These index cards can then be pulled out and placed in the center of the table as they are introduced into a scene.

cally the player who best knows the rules. This player doesn't have any additional authority over the story and plays by the same rules as the rest of the players. Their job will be to write down all of the Facts that are paid for. This record can then be read or passed around when players need to refer back to what's been created. It may be convenient to have another player keep the record when it's the Recorder's turn to play.

Each Component should be given its own section on a blank page with room to add additional Traits during play. Each scene should be given its own section listing which Components are present and describing the key Events in abbreviated bullet-point fashion.

CHAPTER 2:
ESTABLISHING THE TENETS

The first step of any new game of Universalis is to establish what kind of story you and your fellow players desire to tell. Universalis has no established setting and is not designed with any specific genre in mind. It is a toolbox that you can use to craft a story of your own liking through play. But before you begin using any tool, you have to know what sort of project you're using it for. All players will participate in defining a series of Tenets that establish the parameters for the upcoming game.

TENETS

Tenets are Facts that define the game – what type of world it will be set in, what type of story is about to be told in it, how players prefer to play, and what special rules may be used.

At the beginning of the game, the starting player is determined by any means desired (age, seat position, seniority, volunteer, etc.). That player must either pay 1 Coin to propose a game Tenet or pass. Play proceeds clockwise around the table with each player paying 1 Coin to propose a Tenet or passing. Tenets are written down in a list by the Recorder.

Once all of the players are satisfied with the Tenets that have been drafted (i.e. all players have passed), actual play (as described in Chapter 3) begins. This should only occur after enough Tenets have been accepted to give all players a pretty solid idea about what type of game is about to be played and how they (as a group) have consented to play it.

Sometimes it is enjoyable to plunge into a game with only a minimum of prepared Tenets. This usually leads to a very chaotic and often silly, but sometimes extremely liberating and enjoyable, experience. For a more serious and deeper game, players are encouraged to spend as much time as necessary establishing Tenets thoroughly.

A good sign that you have enough Tenets to begin play is when players start trying to develop plot elements via Tenets. Establishing background with Tenets is often useful, but if an actual narrative starts to evolve, the game is clearly ready to

(13)

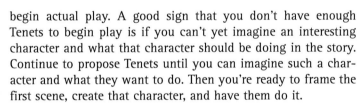

DESIGN NOTE

Universalis requires that all players are creatively engaged and committed to the story being told. The Tenets phase ensures that all players contribute to establishing the structure for that story. Players who actively participate in establishing Tenets are not only demonstrating a commitment to putting forth the effort to play, but are also more likely to be inspired during play because they helped create the framework of the game.

Any players who are not actively participating in creating Tenets may not completely understand the level of creative engagement and initiative successful Universalis play requires. More experienced players should help guide them through the process but it is important that the player's contributions are their own, not merely parroted suggestions from other players. New players must feel comfortable contributing to the game and free to act on their own imagination.

It is not uncommon for a group's first game of Universalis to wind up with a story that's pretty silly, or even an absurd mix of conflicting genres (the "everything but the kitchen sink" game). Universalis asks players to put their creativity to the test in real time to be judged by their peers, and often the safest way to do that is to use humor. Such a game is great for teaching the rules and building a comfort level among the players. To keep future games more focused, try spending more time establishing solid Tenets.

begin actual play. A good sign that you don't have enough Tenets to begin play is if you can't yet imagine an interesting character and what that character should be doing in the story. Continue to propose Tenets until you can imagine such a character and what they want to do. Then you're ready to frame the first scene, create that character, and have them do it.

○ There are three types of Tenets that can be proposed: Story Elements, Social Contract issues, and Rules Gimmicks.

○ You may propose one and only one Tenet on each of your turns, and doing so costs 1 Coin.

This rule applies for the entire game, so that at any time during actual play a player can also spend 1 Coin to propose one

14

new Tenet (and no more than one) on his turn.

This process is called "proposing" a Tenet because the player's choice is not carved in stone. Anything you say or do during the game is subject to being Challenged by another player who disagrees with you or thinks he has a better idea. The Challenge mechanic is explained in Chapter 3 starting on page 34. Unless there is a Challenge, however, your proposal is presumed accepted and becomes part of the structure of the game. In game terms, each accepted Tenet is considered to be a Fact attached to the game itself. It is possible to propose a change to a previously accepted Tenet, but with the original Tenet serving

RULES GIMMICK:
MULTIPLE TENETS

Over the course of many games, one of the most frequently forgotten rules is the rule that limits a player to proposing only one Tenet on their turn. This rule was designed to make sure that all players had an equal opportunity to set the Tenets for the game by limiting each player to just a single idea at a time.

As it turns out some ideas require more than one Tenet to express properly (especially Story Elements involving adding Traits to Components) and so it has become commonplace in most groups to allow players to introduce multiple Tenets on their turn so long as they're related to the same basic idea.

as a Fact, it becomes easier to Challenge the proposed change and prevent it from being accepted (see page 39 for details).

STORY ELEMENTS

Story Elements are used to specify aspects about the upcoming story such as: genre, theme, premise, settings, situations, mood (including atmosphere and tone), and degree of realism. When you propose a Story Element, you're providing direction to the other players as to the sort of story you're interested in. Each Story Element is both a limiting factor, shrinking the range of narration that will be considered appropriate for the game, and also a creative springboard for other players to riff new ideas from.

The Story Elements will provide the structure for the upcoming game, so it is important that all players are jazzed by the ideas presented. Players should be prepared to make full use of

15

the Challenge mechanic, described in the next chapter, to block Tenets that are deal breakers; that is, any Tenets that would prevent you from enjoying the game.

Story Elements may include defining specific characters or setting locations using the rules in Chapter 5 for Components. Players should not begin to have these Components interact, but a powerful character or mood setting location can be a great source of inspiration for later play.

Let's introduce five players who will be part of our ongoing game play examples – Albert, Bob, Christine, Dave, and Ed – who are sitting around the game table in that order. Albert starts off.

> **Albert:** Let's play a science fiction game tonight. [Albert proposes a genre for 1 Coin.]
>
> **Bob:** Ok, but no space ships...I'm sick of space ships. [Bob proposes a limit to the setting for 1 Coin.]
>
> **Christine:** Hmmm, I was actually looking forward to something more fantasy tonight...how about if we do sci-fi, but with a real fantasy flair? [Christine is informally polling the other players about how likely they are to Challenge her upcoming proposal.]
>
> **Albert:** Like what? [Albert's not sure he likes where this is going.]
>
> **Christine:** Well, like that famous quote "Any technology sufficiently advanced is indistinguishable from magic." So we do all of the trappings of sci-fi, but don't worry about all of the actual science making sense, the technology can be more fantastic, more magical, like the people who use it don't really understand how it works. [This exchange is technically referred to as Negotiation in the Challenge mechanic.]
>
> **Bob:** So, just like Star Trek, then. [Everybody laughs.]
>
> **Christine:** Well...
>
> **Ed:** Yeah, we get it, let's go with that and see what happens [Everybody nods in assent so Christine pays 1 Coin, Negotiation was successful, so there was no need for a full Challenge.]

16

Dave: My turn. Let's see, how about we include a lot of animals mixed in with the technology, like how in Star Wars they still ride dewbacks and tauntauns and such. [Nobody Challenges, so Dave pays 1 Coin.]

Ed: Ok, interesting. But here's a twist, the people are all really small, like just a couple inches tall, so the animals they use are just regular size small animals like mice and lizards.

Bob: What, small like Smurfs?!

Ed: Yeah, only really high tech...and not blue with silly hats, of course.

Christine: Ok, but not lizards, I hate reptiles. [Its not Christine's turn, so she isn't establishing this as one of the Tenets of the game world. At this point she's signaling the other players that she's likely to Challenge things involving lizards. She could propose the *no lizards* rule as a Tenet for 1 Coin on her turn.]

Ed: Fine, lizards can be the enemy then or something [Ed pays 1 Coin for the little people. He can only propose 1 Tenet per turn, so he cannot add the *lizards as the enemy* Tenet on this turn, although he likely will in a later turn.]

And so it continues, until the groundwork for the game is completely laid.

SOCIAL CONTRACT ISSUES

The Social Contract is an agreement between the players as to how they want to play the game. Every play group has its own style of play and every player their own desires for how they enjoy experiencing their games and what they hope to get out of them. By discussing these in advance and reaching some consensus about what is and isn't acceptable before play starts, groups can avoid many of the conflicts that lead to group dysfunction. By treating these as explicit game Tenets that are proposed and accepted, the players are formally agreeing to certain boundaries in their play. Such Tenets may include questions of pacing, outside distractions, table talk, and how closely players are expected to adhere to the tropes of a particular genre

17

The Social Contract can be one of the most important aspects of the game. It is not always necessary to define each aspect of the Social Contract as a formal Tenet, although this may be especially desirable if playing with a new group. Many established groups have played with each other so long that the major Social Contract issues are automatically assumed, even if they've never been explicitly stated. Other times, for quick pick-up games that aren't meant to be serious, potential areas of friction can be largely ignored and basic rules of etiquette relied upon. However, even for the most established groups, spending some time talking about the game and how players expect each other to play it can be a valuable exercise.

The group dynamic issues found in the Social Contract are hardly unique to Universalis. They are a fundamental part of any social activity. This dynamic includes all of the inter-social relationships, issues, life experiences, and personal baggage brought to the table by each of the players. These issues then combine and encounter each other during play, in what can be a very volatile mix, in the same manner as they do during any social activity between human beings.

Because each and every one of us has dealt with social issues for our entire lives, we are all intimately familiar with the kinds of things that might adversely affect a social relationship or that might offer wondrous new opportunities for social synergy. However, it can be useful to discuss these issues at the beginning of play to establish where others' sensitivities lie, lines that should not be crossed, and ground rules that will help enhance everyone's enjoyment.

Returning to our example:

Christine: You know how in that other game we were playing with Steve as the GM he used to raise his hand as a signal for everyone else to get quiet and stop kibitzing. I think that worked pretty well. The person whose turn it is should raise their hand to get everyone's attention, and everyone else has to stop gabbing when they do. [1 Coin for a Tenet addressing table talk.]

Dave: And no cell phones. Bob, last week was totally ridiculous, you got like a thousand calls. Really distracting.

(18)

> I say turn all the phones and pagers and stuff off, and we can check our messages at the next break. [1 Coin for a Tenet addressing outside distractions.]

> **Ed:** And no Monty Python jokes...at all...by anyone. [1 Coin for a Tenet that should be in every game ever played.]

RULES GIMMICKS

Rules Gimmick is the term Universalis uses for optional rules created on the fly to address a specific game issue or player concern. Should you wish to develop a situation where no current rule reflects the effects or environment you're after, you have only to introduce a Rules Gimmick to cover it.

A player may wish to create special effects pertaining to the use or effects of die rolls that aren't covered in the basic rules. Gimmicks can be used to add more simulative detail than is found in the usual Complication rules. Any situation where a player wishes to say "if this roll results in X, then Y will happen" is possible within Universalis using Rules Gimmicks. Other special rules may not involve dice at all, and some may change the way the game is played. But, no matter what it is, if the rule isn't already written, players can write it on the fly as a Rules Gimmick.

Gimmicks are introduced like any other Tenet. Pay 1 Coin to define the Gimmick, and if no one Challenges successfully, it's the rule. Players may make suggestions to the rule as part of the Challenge Negotiation process. This can include modifying the way the rule works, asking that it take more than 1 Coin to use, or limiting its use to just this one scene. The proposing player is free to refuse or adopt these as desired, depending on how confident he feels about winning a Challenge.

Over the years, players have invented a large number of Rules Gimmicks, many of which can be found on the Universalis website (www.ramshead.indie-rpgs.com). I've included many of the most popular ones in text boxes throughout these rules as further examples.

> In our ongoing example of play, several diminutive characters were caught in a torrential thunderstorm. It's Albert's turn.

> **Albert:** As a result of the storm, everyone should be soaking wet, so I want to give each of the characters

the Trait *Soaked to the Skin*. But I don't want to pay 1 Coin apiece for all that, because that's just way too expensive for something that should be a pretty obvious outcome from the storm anyway. So I'm going to propose a Rules Gimmick: "Traits describing weather effects can be applied to all characters exposed to the effects for a single Coin." [1 Coin for a Rules Gimmick.]

Ed: I don't know. That seems pretty powerful, you can get a lot of Coins worth of effect pretty cheap that way. [Ed is hinting that he might Challenge the proposed Gimmick.]

Dave: Yeah but it does make sense, I mean it was raining...now everybody should be wet...right? [Dave is voicing support for the Gimmick.]

Bob: It needs some more limits, like it doesn't apply to characters who have the proper protection. [Bob is suggesting a modification and hinting that he'll support Ed's Challenge if he doesn't get it.]

Christine: So you mean that for 1 Coin, every character can be made soaking wet, except for the ones that have a rain coat or an umbrella listed as a Trait? [Christine is asking for clarification on the suggested modification.]

Bob: Yeah, or on a hot day someone could give everyone sunburn except for the ones wearing sun screen.

Ed: Yeah, and the Trait should be able to be removed from everyone with a single Coin too for when enough time has passed and they've dried off. [Ed is suggesting additional modifications to the Gimmick required to win him over.]

Albert: Sounds good, it will work like that. [Albert agrees with the suggestions, modifies his Gimmick accordingly and pays the Coin required to make everyone *Soaked to the Skin*.]

In another example, Christine has just finished narrating

CHAPTER 2: ESTABLISHING THE TENETS

art © 2002, david hedgecock

Thinking fast, the team of meadow heroes escapes the raging forest fire by clinging to the backs of fleeing squirrels.

an exciting scene where the heroes are clinging to the backs of squirrels, racing to escape a forest fire. There are a couple more things she wants to do before closing the scene but she's found she's run out of Coins.

Albert: No problem, how many do you need, Christine?

Christine: Oh, about four should do it I think.

Albert: Here you go.

Dave: Wait a minute, you can't give Coins away like that. It's not in the rules.

Albert: Ok, here's 1 Coin for a Rules Gimmick that says you can loan Coins to another player if that player agrees to pay back double next time they receive Coins...any Challenges? Christine, you agree to that? Great, here are your 4 Coins, pay me back 8 when you get them.

CHAPTER 3: SCENE FRAMING & GAME FLOW

All of the action that takes place in the game occurs within scenes. One player will frame the scene and all players will then have the opportunity to participate in it. Players will narrate the events and action of the scene during their own turn and by interrupting the turns of other players.

REFRESHMENT

Refreshment occurs immediately following the end of each scene. All players receive a set number of Coins from the Bank.

It is suggested that starting groups use 5 Coins as the Refreshment amount, but each group is encouraged to experiment and find an amount they find most appealing (Rules Gimmicks are a great way to handle this).

> Following Christine's earlier scene involving the forest fire and the squirrels, where she used her last 4 Coins to narrate the heroes' harrowing escape across the river, she declared the scene over. She, and each of the other players, then received 5 Coins from the Bank.

FRAMING SCENES

Scenes serve to organize the action of the story into discrete vignettes. A scene is begun by the winner of a closed bid auction and is ended when that player declares it over.

BID FOR NEXT SCENE

As soon as a scene ends, players receive their Refreshment of Coins. They then bid for the privilege of framing the next scene. Each player (including the player whose turn just ended) makes a closed bid by secretly selecting any number of Coins from their Wealth and concealing them in their hand. Bids are then revealed simultaneously. Losing bids are withdrawn, the winning bid remains on the table. It is possible for the same player to frame consecutive scenes if they win consecutive bids.

○ In the event of a tie, the tied player sitting closest to the left of the player who framed the last scene wins.

RULES GIMMICK:
FIRST SCENE REFRESH

Contributed by Roy Penrod

In the core rules, Refreshment occurs at the end of a scene before the next scene begins. This means that there is no Refreshment before the first scene. Players begin the first scene with whatever Coins they have remaining after establishing Tenets (Chapter 2).

With this Gimmick, groups can allow a standard Refresh before the very first scene of a game to give everyone a few more Coins to start actual play with.

Variant: Instead of a standard Refresh, reset each player's Wealth back to its starting value (25 Coins is the default) before the first scene. This will encourage players to really spend Coins to add additional detail to the setting by establishing Tenets, since any Coins not spent will have been wasted.

○ It can be helpful (especially with larger groups) to use a handy prop to signify who the scene framer is. The prop gets passed to whomever wins the bid and serves as a reminder of who has the authority to end the scene.

If no one bids, the first player to the left of the last framing player (i.e. clockwise) is declared the winner and must then bid at least 1 Coin. If this player has no Coins (possible if the group has set Refreshment to zero) proceed to the first clockwise player who does.

Christine ended her scene with the squirrel-riding heroes leaping from branch to branch across a river to safety, and each player received their small Refreshment of Coins. They then bid to see which of them will frame the next scene. Each player secretly selects a number of Coins for their bid and holds them in their hand out over the table. Albert's hand is empty; he bid zero because he doesn't have a good idea for a new scene. Bob bid 4 Coins; he has a pretty good idea he wants to try. Christine bid zero because she doesn't have many Coins, just the few she received from Refreshment (and, in fact, she still owes Albert 8). Dave also bid 4. Ed bids 3.

23

Bob and Dave are tied with a bid of 4 Coins each. Dave is sitting immediately clockwise from Christine, so he wins the tie. Bob and Ed both return their bids to their Wealth. Dave leaves his out on the table to be spent during the upcoming scene.

WINNING THE BID

The player who wins the bid is called the Framing Player. Their winning bid remains in front of them on the table and can be used throughout the scene. Any Coins from this bid that are not used before the scene ends are lost to the Bank.

They have the responsibility of framing the next scene of the story. A scene may be of any duration, from a brief cut to action happening elsewhere that takes only a few minutes of play to an epic climax that is extended over an hour or more with each player taking multiple turns.

The Framing Player must accomplish three tasks. They must: Establish the Location, Set the Time, and Introduce the Components. The Framing Player cannot be Interrupted while they are performing these tasks (although they can be Challenged as usual). This immunity ends as soon as the Framing Player narrates the first Event of the scene.

Having won the bid for turn, Dave now sets about framing the new scene.

Dave: Ok, the scene cuts, and we are now in the central throne room of the Slytheran Queen, sworn enemy of the Meadow People [This establishes the Location and costs 1 Coin. The Slytheran are a race of diminutive reptilian people who serve as the principle villain of the story. Both the Slytheran people and the Queen were Created during earlier play.]

Dave: It's shortly after the heroes escaped from the fire. [Setting the time consecutive to the previous scene costs nothing.]

Dave: The Queen and three of her Generals are discussing plans to invade the Meadow [Introducing characters into the scene costs 1 Coin each. The Queen is an existing character and so brings with her all of her existing Traits. The 3 Generals are new. They cost 1 Coin each to Create

24

them into the scene, which gives them nothing but a basic Role Trait (currently just Generals #1, #2, and #3, see Chapter 5 for further details on Creating Components). Having the characters discuss their plans is actually an Event, which itself costs a Coin. The defining of the first Event ends the framing part of the scene. Dave continues with his turn but can now be Interrupted.]

ENDING THE SCENE

Only the Framing Player can formally end the scene (although they can be Challenged to get them to do so). They can do this any time on their turn (except while being Interrupted) by simply declaring the scene to be over. Following a standard Refreshment, the next scene is then bid for as above. Ending a scene costs nothing.

ESTABLISH LOCATION

○ **Establishing or changing location costs 1 Coin.**

All scenes require a location to occur in. All locations are a type of Component that is Created by the players and can be assigned Traits as described in Chapter 5.

Locations can be changed during a scene by a player merely establishing a new location exactly as above on their turn. Changing locations is not the same thing as starting a new scene. It is appropriate only when a single scene spans across multiple locations (such as during a chase). Characters and Components should remain fairly constant across locations. It is assumed that all Components travel to the new location at no additional cost. Any that do not should be paid to exit (also for 1 Coin). Only Traits from the current location are available to be drawn upon for dice in Complications (see Chapter 6). If the change of location also involves a substantial change in cast, then this is best handled by ending the current scene and beginning a new one.

SET THE TIME

Setting the time costs:

○ Nothing if it follows immediately on the previous scene

○ 1 Coin to set it in the past

○ 1 Coin paid to each other player to set it in the future

25

Unless otherwise stated, each scene occurs either immediately subsequent to the previous one or simultaneously with it (possible if framed at a different location). This is the default and costs nothing. Establishing a time other than these must be paid for.

There are two ways to frame into the past. The first is to frame into the distant past to deal with Events that occurred before the current game began. These are the easiest past frames to accomplish as the player must only ensure he does not establish any Facts which violate what is already known to be Fact (unless he desires to do so and is risking Challenge). The second is to frame the scene back to an earlier point in the game itself. This is a much more advanced technique. If you intend to use it with any frequency you should be certain to maintain your game log very carefully so you have a timeline of scenes and which Components were present in order to preserve continuity.

Framing a scene into the future, however, will limit the Events of other scenes that occur before it chronologically but have yet to be framed. In order to frame a scene into the future the player must pay 1 Coin to each other player in the game as compensation for limiting their future control in this way. For instance, setting a scene five years into the future requires that all characters present in that scene are alive at that time. This limits the other players' ability to narrate the death of any of those characters before then.

During most scenes, time progresses at a normal rate into the future. The time of the scene is not normally changed in mid scene the way a location can be changed. Usually if game time is to be moved substantially forward or is to flash back to the past, a whole new scene or mini scene (see page 32) is framed and an appropriate time set. However, since it is not possible to write rules to cover every possible scene players could wish to invent, this rule can be violated by proposing a Rules Gimmick allowing it to be lifted. For instance a *Time Machine* Component may allow the Controlling player to narrate changes in the time of the scene.

INTRODUCE COMPONENTS

○ It takes 1 Coin to Introduce 1 Component into, or Exit 1 Component from, a scene

All scenes start as collections of Components that are active in it (i.e. a location, characters at that location, and any props that are present). The act of adding a Component to a Scene is called "Introducing" that Component. This costs 1 Coin. If the Component already exists (i.e. has been Created previously) then the 1 Coin pays for its presence in the scene. If the Component has not yet been Created, then it is Created now with that Coin (Creating Components and assigning Traits to them is described in detail in Chapter 5).

Only Components that have been Introduced in this way are present in the scene. Components that have been eliminated from play using the Importance rules cannot be Introduced in a scene set chronologically after the one in which they were eliminated (Importance and Eliminating Components is described in detail in Chapter 5, page 78).

> **GAME PLAY NOTE: SUSPENSE**
> *Contributed by Clinton Nixon*
> The game itself is more suspenseful than most role-playing games. Most RPGs aren't suspenseful at all for the GM - he knows what's going to happen. Even in a heavily narrativist game, he has some ideas, and knows the agendas of his antagonists. Players can read this, by the way - people can be obvious. I've often known what was going to happen in a game because I knew what TV shows the GM watched, or movies he liked, or books he read.
>
> In Universalis, since everyone contributes, no one knows for sure what might happen next. This kicks ass.

The player who Introduced the Component Controls it initially, although Components can change hands during the scene. The Controlling player (and only the Controlling player) can add, remove, or restore Traits to the Component, without originating a Complication. Control of a Component in one scene has no bearing on who Controls that component in a subsequent scene.

Additional characters and props can be Introduced at any time throughout the scene during player turns in this same way, by simply paying a Coin. The Introducing player will have initial Control.

Controlled Components can similarly be Exited from a scene by paying a Coin to have them depart. This departure can be for any narrative reason, but it cannot be permanent. Any Exited Component is available to be reintroduced at any time unless formally Eliminated from play using the rules in Chapter 5.

Players can also spend a Coin to explicitly state a Component

27

RULES GIMMICK:
FADE TO BLACK

The Framing Player may choose to pay 1 Coin when ending a scene to "Fade to Black." Fading to Black prevents the next Framing Player from extending the scene or returning to it at any point in the future.

This may be desirable if the player feels he has ended the scene in a suitably dramatic fashion and doesn't want another player dragging it out.

Like anything else in the game, "Fade to Black" can be Challenged by any player who feels it inappropriate.

as not being in the scene. This may be desirable because another player is free to retroactively place any character not so limited into the scene at a later time. For example, if the Events of a scene included a murder, another player could later frame a scene at a local police precinct where a character (who wasn't explicitly present in the earlier scene) is claiming to be a witness to the crime. Explicitly paying to not have that character present at the scene is a Fact that could be used to assist in Challenging that attempt (or at least Challenge it being true, the character could still lie about having been a witness, but the players would all know that she actually wasn't).

CUTTING BACK TO THE SAME SCENE

Instead of framing a new scene after winning the bid, the Framing Player may elect to continue the action of a previous scene (including the scene just ended) by spending 1 Coin to Establish the Location as that prior scene. If that scene was in the past or the future additional Coins must be spent to Set the Time.

Components that have already been established as being in that location at that time do not have to be reintroduced. In fact, in this situation, it would require Coins to Exit a Component from a scene where it otherwise should be. In other words, everyone and everything that was there in the prior scene is automatically there, for free, in the continuing scene.

○ The Framing Player is considered to have Introduced all of those existing Components into the continuing scene and thus gains Control over all of them regardless of who was in Control of them during that previous scene

In this way scenes can be paused while a new scene cuts to action elsewhere. Then a subsequent scene can simply pay to

GAME PLAY NOTE: ADVICE ON SCENE FRAMING
Contributed by Christopher Bradley

"Universalis is currently my favorite game, but I clicked with it unusually well. I've played a fair bit of it with a fair number of people and noticed that I seemed to come up with scenes much faster and do much meatier scenes than the rest of the players in the group. We asked ourselves why this is happening.

I told them what I did. I thought of a climactic future scene I wanted to see in the story and I used the power of scene framing to work towards it. They weren't doing that. They instead tried to think of "where the story would go from here" given what had just happened, rather than thinking about where they wanted it to go in the future. When they started to think proactively ahead about where they'd like the story to go it was, like, WOW! 1000% change. It was pretty dramatic.

When everyone started Bidding for Scene with an idea of where they wanted to take the story, they also became more likely to Interrupt, Challenge, or Originate Complications during the scene; which I thought was just great. Hitherto, the players had thought these were disturbing someone else's play -- but now they seemed to better understand that everyone's idea for the direction of the story creates a kind of friendly competition. No one's plans had precedence over anyone else's."

A great piece of advice from a long-time player of the game. The dynamic synergy of each player's different ideas for the direction of the story is what makes the game dramatic, suspenseful, and guaranteed to result in a story that no one player would have thought of on their own.

cut back and pick up the action of the first scene from where it was left off with all prior Components included. Note that if this technique is used often, players would be well served to keep careful record of scenes and the Components that were present.

PLAYER TURNS

29

All scenes have a formal beginning and a formal ending. In between there will be many player turns as players take their actions and Interrupt each other to narrate some element of the story. The Framing Player essentially has the first turn, which begins as soon as the scene is framed. When a player does not want or cannot afford to do anything further they end their turn and play proceeds to the next player in clockwise order. Note: ending one's turn is not the same thing as ending the scene.

INTERRUPTION

A player can Interrupt another player's turn by spending 1 Coin to do so. Play passes to the Interrupting player and proceeds clockwise from there when he is done, unless he is also Interrupted.

⭘ **Interrupting a turn costs 1 Coin.**

These rules provide a good deal of structure as to whose turn it is and what they get to do on their turn. However, in practice players will find turns evolve in very free-form fashion. A player may spend some time narrating a scene until a second player Interrupts. That player just adds a single Event and then ends his turn. The next player begins his turn until Interrupted by the fourth, who begins narrating his own ideas, until the first player Interrupts him to start a Complication. In

> ### INTERRUPT PRIORITY
> In the event that multiple Interruptions happen at the same time, precedence is given to the player sitting closest to the Interrupted player's left.
>
> This precedence even trumps players who clearly declared Interruption first. The purpose of this rule is to prevent Interruptions from becoming a speed contest to see who can Interrupt first. Regardless of who's first, the player closest to the current player's left always gets priority.

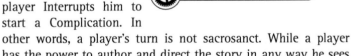

other words, a player's turn is not sacrosanct. While a player has the power to author and direct the story in any way he sees fit during his turn, his turn is always subject to Interruptions by other players seeking to do the same thing. In this way, suspense is maintained because no player can ever really be sure what's about to happen or why.

The player being Interrupted can complete whatever immediate narration he was doing (i.e. he can't be stopped in mid sentence) but

CHAPTER 3: SCENE FRAMING & GAME FLOW

cannot continue with his turn beyond that immediate action. He is, of course, free to spend a Coin to Interrupt and take the turn right back. The only times a player cannot be Interrupted are when they have won the bid for turn and are engaged in framing the scene or while they are narrating the resolution of a Complication using Bonus Coins (See Chapter 6, page 107).

○ The Framing player is immune to Interruption until the location, time, and principal Components present have been announced.

○ Once they narrate the first Event, they are no longer immune.

○ Players narrating with the Bonus Coins they received from resolving a Complication are also immune to Interruption.

Dave has continued to narrate his scene in the Queen's throne room when he is Interrupted by Ed.

Ed: I'm Interrupting you for 1 Coin. [Dave finishes his last thought, but can spend no further Coins.]

Ed: As the planning continues, a scout rushes into the throne room and dismounts to give his report [This costs 1 Coin to Create the scout as a new character with the Role Trait of *Scout*. Note: the cost would have been the same if Ed were Introducing an existing scout character into the scene. Ed could also pay 1 Coin to add a Trait like *Mounted* to the Scout. Some groups may also want to pay 1 Coin for the specific action of the Scout "dismounting" but most groups will tend to treat this as Color (see Chapter 4, page 47, for more on Color and Chapter 5, page 57, for more on Traits.)]

Ed: "My Queen," he says, "the fire was set as per your orders, however, I regret to inform you that we believe the Meadow spies managed to escape across the River" [This costs 1 Coin for the Event of having the scout deliver his report to the Queen and 1 Coin for the Fact about the fire having been set by the Slytheran.]

There are a couple things of note here. First, during Christine's forest fire scene, she had never established the

31

origins of the fire. Ed has interrupted this scene to establish that the fire was intentionally set by the evil Slytheran who will stop at nothing to kill the Meadow People.

Second, since Ed now Controls the Scout and Dave still Controls the Queen (see the section on Control in Chapter 4, page 49), Ed and Dave can speak to each other in the voices of those characters using the Dialog rules (also found in Chapter 4, page 52.)

MINI SCENES

When you take a turn during a scene, you may temporarily change the scene in order to describe events happening elsewhere. Ordinarily, especially if this other scene is to be an elaborate one, you should wait for the current scene to end and then bid enough to win the next scene and describe the events then. However, sometimes the desired scene is too small to be worth bidding many Coins on to ensure winning the bid; and sometimes the information you want to convey would lose its impact if not conveyed immediately. When this is the case, you may make use of a Mini Scene.

> **FRAMING VS. TAKING A TURN**
>
> When you frame a new scene (after winning the bid) you establish location, set the time, and introduce Components. You are immune to Interruption while you do this.
>
> When you take a turn during an existing scene, you do not do these things. Any given scene can consist of multiple turns as play passes around the table or jumps between players due to Interruptions.
>
> A new scene is not framed until the Framing Player ends the current scene and the players bid for the privilege of framing the new one.

A Mini Scene must be Framed exactly as described above for any other scene; this includes immunity from Interruption during the actual Framing. You must Establish Location, Set the Time (most often either concurrently with the main scene, or in the past as a flash back), and Introduce Components.

The Mini Scene must be ended when your turn ends (either by ending it yourself or through Interruption) and there is no Refreshment received for it. Unless the player paid a Coin to Fade to Black, however, the mini scene can be picked up again and continued either as another Mini Scene, or as a regular full scene after bidding.

> Back in the throne room, Ed has ended his turn following the scout's report, so play continues with Albert.

Albert: Ok, I'm declaring a Mini Scene, flashing back to the origin of the forest fire. This scene is playing in the background as the scout delivers his report [This costs 1 Coin for the Location where the fire began, and 1 Coin for setting the scene in the past. The visualization on how the scene would play if this were an actual movie is pure color that makes things interesting but has no cost.]

Albert: Present are a team of Slytheran [1 Coin for Creating the team of Slytheran as a Component plus two more to represent their numbers as a Group Trait (see Chapter 5, page 63, for more details on creating groups as single Components.)]

Albert: ... and Jerek the Sparrow Rider [1 Coin for Introducing Jerek into the scene. Jerek is an existing character who has as a Trait the fact that he was *Exiled by the Meadow People Years Ago.* He also has as a Trait, *Possesses the Sparrow 'Fright'* which he rides. This allows the sparrow (which has been defined as a separate Component) to be Introduced into the Scene automatically for free (see Chapter 5, page 67, for more details on using Traits to express possession.)]

Albert: Jerek observes the Slytheran start the fire and trails them as their scouts follow the fleeing Meadow People heroes. [1 Coin for the Event of Jerek observing the activity, 1 Coin for Introducing the Scouts into the scene, and 1 Coin to follow them. The flight of the heroes has already been described in Christine's earlier scene.]

Albert: That's the end of my turn [Albert ends his turn. He's managed to tie the roguish character Jerek to the events of the story with this scene. Perhaps in another scene one of the players will describe Jerek flying in to give aid to the heroes, potentially earning redemption for his past, as yet unspecified, crimes.]

33

art © 2002, david hedgecock

CHALLENGES AND FINES

Challenges are a way for players to police other players in the game. Challenges can occur for any reason. Anything a player says or does in the game can be Challenged. This can include player behaviors that are not directly game-rule related but are deemed inappropriate. There are two phases to a Challenge, Negotiation and Bidding. In the Negotiation phase, if players can reach an agreeable accord, play can continue virtually uninterrupted. Only if an accord cannot be reached does the Challenge proceed to a Bidding contest.

34

○ A player normally uses challenges on another player's turn to oppose or suggest changes to what the other player is doing.

RULES GIMMICK: MINI INTERRUPTIONS

Contributed by Roy Penrod

In the core rules, if a player wants to add a Trait to a Component when it is not their turn, they must 1) Spend a Coin to Interrupt, 2) Spend a Coin to take Control of the desired Component, and 3) Spend Coins to add the desired Traits; after which the turn progresses to the player on their left, not the player they interrupted. This works extremely well as a rule to keep a tightly regimented and organized formal turn structure, but can be rather expensive and cumbersome when someone just gets a great idea for a Trait and wants to get it into play. As groups gain experience with the rules, they often find that the extra organization isn't always necessary or desired, and often the first Gimmicks a play group will come up with involve loosening the turn structure.

This Gimmick allows a player to temporarily Interrupt another player for free and temporarily Take Control of a Component for free in order to spend Coins to add desired Traits. Once the Traits have been added, Control reverts to the previous controlling player and the Turn returns to the player who was Interrupted (unlike a full Interruption). At any time in this process, if the player who was Interrupted doesn't like the Traits being added he can cancel the Mini Interruption and force the other player to use the full formal Interrupt and Control rules.

Combining this with the Friendly Control Gimmick (page 52) and the Free Dialog Gimmick (page 54) really loosens the turn structure up, but can also lead to greater anarchy for players who aren't ready for it.

NEGOTIATION

A Challenge is a way for a player to police other players in the game. This can be done with a formal declaration of Challenge or be as simple as "Hey wait, that doesn't make much sense." Challenges can also be used to offer suggestions for a different approach that the Challenger would like better, such as, "Hey, that's great, but I think it would work better if Jack just stared him down coldly rather than start a brawl like that."

If the acting player alters their play in a manner acceptable to the Challenger, then the Challenge ends and the acting player continues their turn. Or, if the acting player can convince the Challenger that their way is better, then the Challenger can drop the Challenge. In this way, all players can take interest and collaborate in a scene, or they can rein in players who are straying from the Social Contract or a desired game mood, etc, in a non-disruptive manner.

The challenged player only pays for the final result of the Negotiation. Any Coins spent on statements that were withdrawn are recovered.

> In an earlier scene, the party of Meadow Heroes had been crossing a pond in a makeshift canoe made out of a curled dry leaf and a couple of twigs, when Bob Originated a Complication involving a snapping turtle. Bob won the dice roll and used his bonus Coins to narrate the turtle overturning the boat and then snapping one of the characters, Turk Reigns, in half and devouring him (by spending Coins equal to Turk's Importance to Eliminate him as explained in Chapter 5, page 79.)
>
> **Ed:** Wait a minute, I like Turk! He's a pretty cool character. Besides, he's a special forces operative and the team needs him to get through to the Slytheran nest.
>
> **Bob:** It's okay to have characters die. Besides, he has a silly name and deserves to get eaten. That's what happens when the Complication dice roll big. You should have built a bigger Dice Pool if you didn't want to lose. [Here Bob is suggesting that if Ed was so worried about characters dying, he should have fought harder to win the Complication with the snapping turtle – sound advice Ed would do well to remember.]
>
> **Ed:** How about this? The turtle snaps at Turk, but given his Trait of *Split Second Reflexes* he manages to jam his *XR-27 Hyperblast Rifle* (another Trait) in the turtle's jaws, barely escaping. [Since play is not currently in a Complication, Turk's reflexes don't have any direct mechanical impact here, but Ed is using them to justify how Turk manages to avoid death at the last minute. If he can convince the other players that such a narrow escape is more dramatic than just

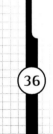

being eaten, *and* in keeping with the character, he might get Bob to back down.]

Bob: Ok, but the turtle snaps the rifle in half and Turk has to cross that Trait off his sheet [It's removed per the rules in Chapter 5, page 82. Since Bob and Ed have come to an accord, the cost for the Complication resolution is recalculated to account for Ed's suggested events. Bob pays the requisite Coins for the new outcome instead of his original suggestion and game play continues normally.]

BIDDING

If the acting player refuses to make changes and the Challenger wishes to insist, then the Negotiation has failed and the Bidding begins. The Bidding is a process by which all players in the game get to rule on the outcome of the Challenge by spending Coins to support whichever player they desire.

Bidding begins with the Challenger, who must bid at least 1 Coin. If they are not willing to do so, then the Challenge immediately ends and the acting player continues their turn. The Bidding then progresses clockwise, with the exception that the player who is being Challenged goes last. Each player in turn bids 1 or more Coins in favor of either the Challenger or the Challenged, or they can pass. Alternatively, a player could bid at least 1 Coin to start a different solution of their own, giving the other players a new option to bid for.

The Bidding continues in this manner until no player wishes to add any further Coins. The Coins are counted and the side with the most support wins. Ties go to the player being Challenged, or, if the tie is between two Challengers, to the option that was started first.

○ If the Challenged player wins, they do not have to change the Challenged item. That item is immune to further Challenge, and they continue their turn.

○ If the Challenger wins, then whatever statements were Challenged do not take effect and the acting player gets those Coins back. They must then be used to pay for whatever the winning Challenger's version of the statement is (if any). If the winning version would cost more Coins then the acting player had originally spent,

(37)

the winning Challenger must make up the difference out of their Challenge Bid or their own Wealth. If they cannot, then whatever is not paid for doesn't happen. The acting player continues with his turn.

○ All Coins bid from any side go to the Bank

RULES GIMMICK: KEEP LOSING CHALLENGE BIDS

Contributed by Mike Holmes

In the Core rules, all Coins bid in a Challenge are considered spent and returned to the Bank regardless of who wins. This rule is in play to counter the "puffing" strategy common in auction games where a player who doesn't really want to win bids up the price for another player who does.

However, some groups have found that since you stand to lose both the Challenge and a sizeable number of Coins you may be less likely to back down. This could lead to unnecessary bidding wars once both parties have too much invested to afford to lose. With this Gimmick you allow one party to concede and recover their bid, making them more likely to back out rather than fight to the bitter end.

Variant: as a compromise solution, allow those who withdraw from a Challenge to recover one half of their bid.

Suppose Bob was not willing to accept Ed's suggestion.

Bob: No way, Turk's buying it.

Ed: Okay, then I guess I'll have to Challenge that. [1 Coin. From here it goes around the table.]

Albert: Doesn't matter to me either way, I'm not spending anything.

Christine: I don't like the idea of a main character dying so early. Ed's solution sounds exciting enough to me, so I Bid 1 Coin for Ed. [Bob as the Challenged party gets to go last.]

Dave: Silly name, eh? I named Turk. I don't think it's such a silly name, 1 Coin for Ed.

Bob now sees 3 Coins arrayed against him. If he had a lot of extra Coins, he'd Bid 4 and see how far the others are willing to go. He really wants Turk dead. But he doesn't have that many Coins and it's hard to overcome three other players in a Challenge by himself, so he resigns...planning to try to kill Turk off again later.

Ed's version of events wins out and the resolution cost is recalculated. Bob recovers the Coins he'd spent to overcome Turk's Importance in order to kill him and instead uses as many of those Coins as necessary to narrate the scene with the escape and the broken rifle instead.

Bob then continues with his turn, and the 3 Bid Coins are paid to the Bank.

USING FACTS IN CHALLENGES

Every Trait and every Event in the game also serves as a Fact. A Fact is defined as any piece of information that a player has established in the game and has paid a Coin for. That last is important. If a Coin wasn't spent on it, it's not considered to be a Fact. The term Fact can be used interchangeably with Trait or Event or Tenet in many cases, as all three involve a player making a statement and paying 1 Coin for it.

In game terms, the effect of a Fact is to give additional leverage during Challenges. If an established Fact is being contradicted, any Coins spent in defense of that Fact (i.e. opposing the contradiction) are doubled for purposes of determining the winner of the Challenge, thereby making the violation more expensive.

This is intentionally not the same thing as saying a Fact can never be violated. Reality and stories are rife with examples of things that were believed to be true until discovered otherwise, or two different groups fanatically believing contradictory truths.

Therefore, a Fact is only absolutely true until: 1) someone pays for a different Fact that contradicts it, *and* 2) no one successfully Challenges that contradiction. For example: Naomi may have been established as Sebastian's daughter; but sometime later a player decides to frame a scene "revealing" that she is actually Drake's daughter. If someone Challenges this statement, the Challenge is made with the weight of the original Fact behind it, but if no one does, then the new "Fact" takes effect.

Note that the new Fact does not always replace the old Fact,

art © 2002, david hedgecock

although it likely does in the above example. Instead, the incident of violation can be described as an exception to the Fact which otherwise remains in place rather than being repealed entirely. For instance: take the Fact "Nothing can travel faster then the speed of light." If someone then narrates a discovery that permits faster than light travel, it doesn't necessarily eliminate the original Fact. Instead the Fact could be modified to become "Nothing can travel faster then the speed of light, except the PanGalactic Hyperform Transducer Drive." This still leaves the original Fact largely in place to Challenge other contenders.

40

Determining whether a Fact is replaced or modified occurs during a Challenge as part of the conditions of the Challenge. Often, a player who is willing to accept a modification rather than insist on total replacement may find they can avoid a full Challenge altogether.

Any player can attempt to bring a Fact into play during a Challenge, but if there is any doubt as to its applicability, a majority vote of players can determine it. If a player doesn't agree with the decision, the outcome of the vote can itself be Challenged.

○ If the Challenge involves a Fact that is being contradicted, Coins spent in defense of that Fact count double.

○ The Fact that is being Challenged can not be used to defend itself.

○ If there's any doubt that a Fact applies, majority vote carries. If the vote ties the Fact is considered to apply.

Back during the forest fire scene, before the heroes managed to escape on the backs of squirrels, Dave took a turn where he narrated several things; one of which was Marissa Tournou (one of the characters) being caught by the flames and severely burned. Christine Challenged that narrative by pointing out that one of Marissa's Traits was *Flame Retardant Jump Suit*. If Dave had pressed the issue and tried to burn Marissa anyway, any Coins spent opposing him would have had their value doubled because the majority of players ruled that the suit constituted a Fact protecting Marissa from fire.

Ed entered into the negotiations and suggested that a fair compromise would be a Rules Gimmick requiring Dave to pay double Coins for whatever effects he wanted the burns to have since the suit was only flame retardant, not flame proof, and so would not give complete protection.

Ultimately Dave avoided going to bidding, by instead narrating Marissa being surrounded by flames, but, thanks to the suit, emerging singed but unharmed.

41

FINES

Instead of, or following, a Challenge, a player can ask that a Fine be levied. Fines should be reserved for egregious behaviors or abuses, which are chronic, have not been solved through Negotiation, and are detracting from the enjoyment of others. The amount of the Fine will generally be fairly trivial. The point of a Fine is not to punish but to gauge the sentiment of the other players. A player who finds the other players united in levying a Fine has been formally requested to alter their behavior.

If a Fine is requested, both sides state their case and then all players vote thumbs up (yes, a Fine should be levied) or thumbs down (no Fine is necessary).

○ If the number of thumbs up is higher, the accused pays Coins equal to the thumbs up to the Bank for his undesirable behavior.

○ If the number of thumbs down is higher then the accuser pays Coins equal to the thumbs down to the Bank for unnecessarily asking for a Fine.

○ If the thumbs are tied, there is no Fine levied against either party.

In an earlier scene, Albert had described an aviary where the Meadow People keep swallows to use as mounts.

Dave: What is the airspeed velocity of an unladen swallow?

Ed: Monty Python violation! I call for a fine.

Four thumbs immediately go up from the players. Dave sheepishly acknowledged his faux pas by putting up his own thumb as well and paying 5 Coins to the Bank.

CHAPTER 4: NARRATING THE SCENE

D uring the course of a scene, players will wind up controlling various characters and narrating what those characters are doing. When characters controlled by different players interact, the players may converse with each other by role-playing the character's dialog. If characters controlled by different players wind up in conflict, the normal scene progression described in Chapter 3 will pause and the conflict will be played out using dice according to the Complication rules found in Chapter 6.

NARRATION AND EVENTS

At the start of the game, you may well have only the vaguest idea of a plot. Most of your time will be spent enjoying the creativity of your fellow players (and they yours). This will likely result in numerous characters whose agendas are initially vague and whose purpose in the story is unclear. There will potentially be many small subplots that may seem entirely arbitrary and unrelated. This is a normal feature of early play, which, in many ways (especially for new players), resembles a brainstorming session that sometimes appears to be all over the place. As the game progresses, you should be looking for ways to tie these disconnected plots together and ascribe motivations and background to sketchy characters in order to make them work. It is a fact of the game that these disparate things exist. Trying to figure out how they are related and why they all belong together in the same story is typically how the plot of the story gets "uncovered."

Late in the game, you should be developing an idea of what you ultimately want to see happen to the major characters in the story and then start paying for the Events and Complications necessary to make it happen and bring the game to closure. The other players should have their own ideas in that regard as well, and the intersection of their ideas and yours (both collaboratively and competitively) is what drives the game forward and makes it fun.

You develop the story by narrating the action of the scene during your turn. As you are speaking, any nouns that you say

43

RULES GIMMICK:
AFFECTING MULTIPLE COMPONENTS WITH THE SAME EVENT

At times Events can get pretty costly. Take the sentence "John hides from the burglar." Assuming John and the burglar already exist in the scene, this takes 1 Coin. But now assume that John, his wife, their three kids, and their dog (who all already exist in the scene) want to hide from the burglar. In the core rules this would take 6 Coins, one for each Component. If there was more than 1 burglar to hide from, the cost would increase even more dramatically.

Using this Gimmick, a player could say, "John's family hides from the burglars" as a 1 Coin Event and cover all of the family members and multiple burglars. It's recommended that this Gimmick be paid for separately each time it used.

Advanced Design Note: This Gimmick is the conceptual equivalent of the players having created John's Family as its own Component, making each of the family members possessions of the family, and then paying for the event "Johns Family hides" which would automatically (using the rules for possessions) apply the event to each of the family members as well. See Chapter 5 for more on Creating Components.

are potential Components for the game. If a named Component isn't already a part of the scene, 1 Coin will Introduce it so it can take part in the action, or, if it doesn't yet exist, 1 Coin will Create it.

Any adjectives you say are potential Traits. Whatever noun the adjective refers to is the Component the Trait is assigned to. 1 Coin can buy 1 Trait for 1 Component. Nouns can also be Traits of other Nouns if they are too minor to be worth Creating separately. Components and Traits are discussed in detail in Chapter 5.

Any verbs or adverbs that you say are potential Events. A typical sentence consists of an Event, a Component causing the Event, a Component experiencing the effects of the Event and potentially several Traits related to the Components. Events also cost 1 Coin and, like everything else in the game, once the Coin is spent (if it is not Challenged) it becomes a Fact that the Event occurred.

CHAPTER 4: NARRATING THE SCENE

For example, during a particularly harrowing scene, our intrepid Meadow team is attacked by a buzzer. It is Christine's turn:

Christine: Marissa shoots the buzzer in the wing with her laser pistol.

In this sentence the Event is the shot, Marissa is the Component causing the Event, the Buzzer is the Component receiving the effect of the Event and *Shot in the Wing* is a New Trait purchased for the Buzzer representing that effect. *The Laser Pistol* is an existing Trait of Marissa's.

Assuming both Marissa and the buzzer were already present in the scene and Controlled by Christine when she made the statement, the total cost of this sentence is 2 Coins, 1 for the Event of the shot, and 1 for the Trait of the buzzer's injury. If Marissa didn't already have *Laser Pistol* as a Trait, then it would take a third Coin to give her one. If Christine didn't control the buzzer, then this statement would Originate a Complication.

○ Events Cost 1 Coin, which includes any or all of the following elements:

   1) a single action or effect,

   2) a single Component performing the action or effect,

   3) a single Component receiving the action or effect.

Events include: actions performed, conversations held, emotions felt, ideas thought, environments changed, beliefs challenged, and anything else that can be thought of as an action or an activity.

HOW MUCH DOES IT COST?

Exactly how much a given sentence of narration should cost may not be immediately obvious. Because of the near infinite number of potential Events that can be narrated, there is no way to write rules to cover each possibility specifically. What is clear is that some definitions of an Event are far too narrow and clumsy to be fun, while other definitions of an Event are far too broad and would allow players to accomplish too much with a single Coin.

45

One way to deal with this is to establish during the Tenets phase a general consensus on how your group plans to define the scope of events and Traits.

Another way is to allow the scope to be established organically during play. Whenever you state an Event or establish a Trait for a Component and pay your Coin, you are making an implicit assertion that the scope of your Event or Trait should cost only 1 Coin. If no other player disagrees, then the scope of that narration is deemed to be acceptable to your group. If another player believes it is not acceptable (because they think it's too narrow or not narrow enough) they can Challenge. In the Negotiation phase, players can discuss what they feel is or isn't an appropriate scope for that particular Event, and can suggest how many Coins they think it should cost (i.e. how many individual Events are really embedded in what the narrator said).

Either through Negotiation or Bidding (or no Challenge at all) the issue gets resolved, the Coins get paid, and all players have a new data point to help judge where the narration parameters are in the future. The bottom line is, no matter where your group sets the threshold for the scope of a single Event or Trait, if you're having fun, its set at the right level.

This is why in the first chapter we made a point of saying that each play group must determine its own level of Coins to start the game with and to recover via Refreshment.

> Returning to the Example "Marissa shoots the buzzer in the wing with her laser pistol."
>
> Above we established that the shot is the Event, Marissa is the Component causing the Event, and the buzzer is the Component receiving it. The pistol in this case merely justifies the narration. Marissa can't shoot the buzzer without having something to shoot it with.
>
> However, some play groups may argue that there are really 2 Events implicit in this sentence: "Marissa fires the pistol," costing 1 Coin, and "the pistol shoots the buzzer," costing another Coin.
>
> This interpretation is probably far too nitpicky to make for an enjoyable game for most groups, but there will certainly be situations that arise during play , which could be defined equally well in different ways like

this. Often, it will not be clear when one interpretation is better than another. It is up to the individual play group to determine to what degree they wish to subdivide Events into smaller and smaller atomic units. After all, another group may argue that the sentence is really four implicit Events: "Marissa moves her finger," "her finger pulls the trigger," "the trigger discharges the pistol," and "the pistol shoots the buzzer."

The appropriate level of starting Wealth and rate of Refreshment for your group depends highly on whether you see the above sentence as costing 1 Coin or four.

COLOR

Not every statement you make must be paid for with Coins. You are free (and indeed encouraged) to embellish your narrative with colorful detail. Note, however, that only those statements that are explicitly paid for carry the weight of Fact. The act of paying for a statement or flavorful description gives it special significance that it otherwise wouldn't have. In game terms, it has become a Fact.

An easy way to judge when something should be paid for is the written record test. If a player says something that should be recorded in the game log so it gets remembered and can be referred to and used by other players in the future, it's worth paying a Coin for. If a Coin isn't paid, it doesn't get written down and if someone else forgets about it, or chooses to ignore it, tough.

OTHER DETAILS

○ Other details cost 1 Coin as for any Fact.

Other details like "why" and "how" can be added to a scene exactly like purchasing any Fact. In many cases the why is implicit and the how is demonstrated by the Events: the bad guys attacked because they are bad guys, the earthquake happened because it is a force of nature, etc. Other times a player may wish to explicitly state the "why." The Event may have involved the betrayal of a trusted friend. The player may want to illuminate the reasons behind the betrayal, and this can be done, just as for any other Fact, by spending Coins.

47

A good character is defined by their motivations and style as much as they are by any physical description or list of abilities.

GAME PLAY NOTE: MORE ON COLOR

Color is an important concept in the game. Everything you say in the game starts out as Color until you pay a Coin for it to cement it as Fact. Accordingly, anything you don't pay a Coin for is just Color and therefore not Fact. Because it is not Fact, it doesn't have any mechanical effect in the game. Color is never written down, can never be Drawn upon for dice in Complications, and gives no leverage in a Challenge.

What Color does do is allow you to give interesting flavorful descriptions and narratives without breaking the bank. You shouldn't feel like you have to speak in abbreviated bullet points to avoid spending too many Coins. You can say anything you want, it just isn't Fact unless it's paid for.

Color can be completely ignored during future play as if it was never said. Other players may Challenge to get you to pay for a statement if they think it is too important to be left as Color, particularly if it would be disruptive to ignore in the future. Color isn't a license to direct the game's events for free.

One use of Color is to mention items that you want as Traits but instead of paying for them now, you wait until later when you want to use them. Of course, by that time, other Facts may have been added that render that Color obsolete. Also, if other players start to take the game in an undesired direction, it may be too late to purchase the Facts needed to help Challenge them.

Adding "whys" (motivations) and "hows" (style) to your narration will help deepen the character and ensure that other players follow your lead in how you want them played.

Sometimes, however, you will not want to explicitly state the "whys" and "hows." These may be left to be explained by another player in a future scene in a way completely unexpected by the initial player. In this way, suspense can be preserved in a game where the players have total power to author the story. For example, a mafia hit man just kicked in the door and attempted to off one of the game's principal characters. Why? We don't know. The player framing that scene never said. But at some point, unless the players want to leave a rather glaring loose-end in their story, somebody is going to have to come up with a justification and frame a scene accordingly. Until then all of the players are left wondering "why the heck is the mafia trying to kill this guy?"

Similarly, consider a scene framing a secret meeting between an agent and his underworld contact. Another player introduces a Complication (described in Chapter 6) where government counter-espionage forces attempt to apprehend the characters. How did the government know about that meeting in order to crash it? We don't know. The player creating the Complication may not even know. But answering that question will provide some player with great grist for a future scene. Could the agent's contact have betrayed him?

CONTROL

You Control any Component that you Introduce into a scene (either existing or newly Created). This Control does not last beyond the end of the scene. When a new scene is framed, the Framing Player gains Control of whichever Components they Introduce.

You can narrate Events that affect, manipulate, alter, or even destroy any Component which is under your Control (paying the appropriate cost in Coins, of course). You may add Traits or remove them from a Component you Control. You may not directly do these things to any Component that is not under your Control.

There are three things you can do as a player with a Component that is not currently under your Control:

AN IMPORTANT NOTE ABOUT CONTROL

When thinking about Components, it is important to distinguish between Controlling them vs. Creating them.

There are two ways of gaining Control over a Component during a scene. Either you Introduced that Component into the scene, or you took it over from another player (by paying 1 Coin).

Creating a Component does not confer any special advantage regarding Control. If you Introduced the Component into a scene by Creating it from scratch, then you have Control over it by way of the Introduction. However, Control in subsequent scenes is determined irrespective of who initially Created the Component.

Who Created the Component has no mechanical impact on the game.

1. Target it with a Complication or, if already involved, Draw Upon one or more of its Traits to add dice to one of the Dice Pools in the Complication.

2. Take it Over so you now have Control.

3. Engage it in Dialog (if it's capable of such).

COMPLICATIONS

Players are free to narrate any actions that are taken by any Component under their control, and they can apply any effect (including adding, removing, or restoring Traits) to any Component that they Control. However, if they attempt to involve a Component that they do not Control in any of these things, they've Originated a Complication. Complications are described in Chapter 6.

Complications can also be the result of another player placing an Obstacle into the scene. This can happen any time a player describes an Event involving his own Components that another player wishes to turn into a Complication (typically to represent how difficult that Event is). The interfering player can Buy Dice representing the difficulty involved, which the current player must roll against in order to narrate the outcome as they desire. Note that Buying Dice for an Obstacle is conceptually identical to (but procedurally much simpler than): Creating a new Component to represent the Obstacle, buying Traits for it, and then having that Component (which you Control) interact with the targeted Component (which you do not).

> In a later scene, Christine Introduces Princess Altia for 1 Coin. The Princess is an existing character who has been shown to be a friend of the Meadow People and is secretly in love with one of the main characters. Christine wishes to have her desperately try to convince her mother to call off the aggression, so she decides to Originate a Complication between the Princess (Controlled by Christine) and the Queen (Controlled by Dave). Both players will for a dice pool by using applicable Traits present in the scene, or by buying them. Other players, Controlling other characters, can participate as desired. The dice are rolled, and the winner of the roll will get to narrate the outcome as they see fit

(by receiving a significant number of bonus Coins from the Bank). This is explained in detail in Chapter 6.

It's important to note that what's at stake is which player gets to describe the event, not which character "wins" the contest. Since the assault on the Meadow People has become the focal event of the story, Christine, in this example, has no intention of having Princess Altia convince her mother to call it off. Even though Christine is Controlling Altia and Altia wants the assault called off, Christine does not. If she wins, Christine plans on narrating a suitably dramatic scene between mother and daughter, perhaps buying some new Traits for them and setting up a future source of conflict. Also, since she's still low on Coins, she hopes to use the Complication to generate a little extra Wealth for herself. See Chapter 6 for more details.

TAKE OVERS

○ Control of a Component can be taken from another player by paying 1 Coin.

Control can change hands multiple times in a scene in this manner. It is possible for Control to be immediately taken back (also for 1 Coin), and two players intent on Controlling the same Component may spend Coins back and forth until one player yields. Note that this is very similar to the Challenge mechanic explained in Chapter 3. Players are essentially Challenging one another for Control.

It does not have to be your turn in order to Take Over a Component, nor does taking over a Component make it your turn. In fact, a common use is to Take Over a Component during another player's turn for the express purpose of setting up a Complication. In this use, a Take Over can occur after a player has declared an Event or activity but before it has been functionally carried out. By Taking Over a Component involved at that time, the player has turned the Event or activity into a Complication.

Continuing with the throne room scene from Chapter 3, it is now Bob's turn. He decides to Take Over the character General #2 for 1 Coin. Control of this character now passes from Dave, who'd originally Introduced him, to Bob.

DIALOG

Much of the action in Universalis is described in the third person, including conversations like "Joe asks the bartender where he might find Tom Slick." This is common practice in novels where not every word a character speaks is actually said inside of quotation marks. However, there may be times when an actual dialog between characters in first person is dramatically important or just entertaining ("No Luke, *I* am your father."). This rule allows for that.

Normally, when you attempt to interact with or manipulate a character you don't control, the result would be a Complication. However, if the interaction involves a character you do control attempting to speak with a character you don't, Dialog can be the result instead. Note that if the player Controlling the other character doesn't desire dialog, they can force the Event into Complication and the winner can narrate the conversation in the third person as desired. However, if both players are willing, Dialog can be a powerful story tool. Players are free to Take Over characters and enter into Dialog in the same way as they'd Take Over Components to cause a Complication. Players may even ask for volunteers to Take Over a Component that they're currently in Control of in order to engage in Dialog (see also the Friendly Control Gimmick in the sidebar).

The rules of Dialog are simple. A player initiates Dialog as an Event for 1 Coin and can end it at any time and continue with his ordinary turn. If the other character still has more to say, that player can, of course, Interrupt and use his turn to start up the Dialog again. Other activity (such as describing Events going on around the conversation) can be narrated by the player who's

RULES GIMMICK: FRIENDLY CONTROL

Contributed by Kirt Dankmyer

Whoever Controls a component can cede Control at any time to another player, at no cost to anyone. This allows players to give characters to other players for the purpose of more readily establishing dialog or to more readily set up situations for Complications (see Chapter 6).

Variant: Anyone can Take Control of any Component on their turn for no cost. If the current Controller objects, then the player must pay for Control as normal.

52

currently speaking without breaking the Dialog. Essentially, in game terms, each back and forth exchange of dialog is treated as a free Interruption.

After that, each player is free to speak in the voice of the character they're Controlling, in first person, responding to the conversations as they believe the character would. Much of what is said will not have to be paid for and the players are free to converse. However, significant items that are said should be purchased as Facts. Note that if a character says "the treasure can be found on Castaway Island" the relevant Fact is not that the treasure can be found on Castaway Island, but that the character said it could be found there. The character could be mistaken or lying. See the "Other Details" section earlier in this Chapter for more ideas about what might be worth paying for during Dialog.

Note: because of the potential for powerful story development, it is suggested (although not required) that other players avoid Interrupting in the middle of a first person Dialog, unless it is particularly dramatic to do so.

art © 2002, david hedgecock

Having taken over General #2, Bob decides to enter into Dialog with the Queen, who is still Controlled by Dave. The scout character, also present in the scene, is still Controlled by Ed.

Bob: General Frederich von Stuben addresses the Queen [The *General* Trait has already been bought as a Role for this character by Dave, here Bob is assigning a proper name to him to replace the generic placeholder *#2*. This costs 1 Coin.]

Bob: Oh, by the way, we should all use Prussian-sounding names for the Slytheran [This can be considered to be a Tenet of the game that "Slytheran have

RULES GIMMICK: FREE DIALOG

Contributed by Bob McNamee

In the core rules, having a character begin talking to another character is an Event just like having the character run down the street or shoot a gun. It therefore costs 1 Coin. With this Gimmick, to encourage first person conversations between players, that cost is waived. Dialog can be initiated between any characters for free. Any Facts that arise as the result of the conversation must be paid for normally.

Combine this with the Friendly Control Gimmick for games in which character conversations are to be featured.

Prussian names." it costs 1 Coin and, as always, can be Challenged.]

Bob: General Frederich, being quite *Prudent* and a *Master Planner*, [These two Traits cost 1 Coin each.] says "My Queen, I strongly urge you to reconsider this plan. If those Meadow Spies manage to report back, the enemy will be waiting for us. Their defenses are strong, we need more time to prepare." [The plan the General refers to was part of Dave's narrative earlier in the scene. The Meadow Spies are, of course, the heroes who've managed to escape across the river, and the strong defenses were established earlier in the story. Since nothing new is being introduced, there is no additional cost. Dave, however, can reply as the Queen.]

Dave: "Rubbish, the Meadow People are weakling cowards, we will overwhelm them and drive them from the forest." [Again, nothing new in the dialog, but Dave decides to buy the Traits *Proud* and *Reckless Arrogance* for the Queen to describe her attitude. He could also buy *Believes the Meadow People to be Weakling Cowards* as a Trait but decides to leave that as a given.]

Bob: "My Queen, if we but wait, the Meadow People will become complacent and we can strike with full surprise."

Dave: "If we strike now we will have full surprise! What side of the river did the spies end up on?" [Dave looks expectantly at Ed, who is currently playing the Scout.]

Ed: "The north side, my Queen." [Since the exact compass direction had not been explicitly stated in the earlier scene being referred to, Ed is free to add the information as he desires. Thinking fast, he remembers that the nest of the Slytheran is to the north of the Meadow, so by placing the heroes on the north side of the river, he has cleverly given them another obstacle to cross before they can get back home. He pays 1 Coin for this new Fact.]

Dave: "Excellent." Now addressing General #1, the queen says, "Make sure those spies don't make it back to the Meadow in time to raise the alarm."

Dave: The General, being unquestioningly loyal, says, "As you command, my Queen." He then clicks his heels together smartly and leaves to carry out the order. [Here Dave has engaged in Dialog with General #1, who is also under his Control, so he is free to fill in both sides of the conversation. Dave pays 1 Coin to make the order official and 1 Coin to exit General #1 from the scene. He also pays 1 Coin to add the Trait *Unquestioningly Loyal* and another for the Trait *Dressed Smartly* to General #1]

Dave: "General von Stuben, I'll hear no more of delays, make ready the Doom Cannons." [Here Dave addresses Bob and pays 1 Coin for the *Doom Cannons,* an intimidating-sounding weapon that, as yet, no one knows anything about because Dave just made them up.]

Bob: "As you command, my Queen." [Bob says, clueing in to how Dave wants the queen addressed, based on Dave's earlier dialog with himself.]

GAME PLAY NOTE: PLAY THE CHARACTERS

Universalis gives players tremendous ability to make big-picture story decisions about plot, theme, setting, and the cast of characters. Because of this you must make a special effort not to neglect your most important duty as a player: to play the characters.

You are not assigned specific characters which you and you alone will play. Rather, who is currently playing any particular character will change frequently throughout the game using the rules for Control above. But while they may not be yours for the entire game, they are yours for as long as you have Control of them. Thus, try to portray these characters to your fellow players.

You are responsible for what those characters think, what they feel, how they act, and how they react. Like an improv actor, you must give your fellow players something to work with. If characters are interacting, you can use the Dialog rules to hold conversations in your character's voice. As other players narrate activity in a scene you must represent the characters you Control. Interrupt the other players in order to defend your character's agenda. Use the Complication rules to force moments of decision. Take Over characters to portray them to your vision. Look for opportunities where the competing agendas of characters come into conflict and have your character act and react appropriately.

Uniquely, since you won't be the only player controlling the character during play, you'll have the other players' portrayals to inform your performances. Sometimes other players will portray a character differently than you envisioned. This can be an opportunity to have your understanding of a character deepened. Appreciate the nuances brought by your fellow players, and adjust your vision of them accordingly. If you want others to portray a character a certain way in the future, be sure to purchase the appropriate combination of Traits (as explained in the next chapter) to define them. If you are certain you don't like another player's portrayal, Challenge them.

Further, keep in mind that characters are just one type of Component and you will be Controlling those other Components just as you Control characters. You will find yourself portraying buildings, vehicles, animals, organizations, even entire ideologies. You'll play them differently than you would an actual character, but play them you will.

CHAPTER 4: NARRATING THE SCENE

CHAPTER 5:
CREATING COMPONENTS

Previously in these rules, we've discussed how Components are created by spending Coins and how Traits can be added to Components for 1 Coin each. This chapter will delve into the steps of Creating a Component in greater detail.

There are three broad types of Components: characters, locations, and props (people, places, and things). Characters are the most important Components of any story and include great heroes, evil villains, anti-heroes, average Joes, and the supporting cast, all the way down to legions of extras. Locations can be thought of as stage sets. They are the backdrops for the action. Props are everything else. They can be physical objects, like a car or sword or valuable oil painting. They can also be intangibles like religions, ideologies, organizations, etc. Basically, if it is a noun, it can be Created as a Component in the game.

TRAITS

Each Component is defined by a set of Traits. A Component does not exist in the game until a Trait has been purchased for it. Traits are Facts purchased for Components, and as such are the basic building blocks of the game world. Anything that is notable or significant about a Component can be defined as a Trait. *Strong*, *Likes the Ladies*, or *Devout Buddhist* can all be Traits for a character. Likewise a river can be *Deep* and *Cold*, a sword *Perfectly Balanced*, a bar could be *The Place Where Everybody Knows Your Name*. Traits can be virtually any word or phrase that describe a feature or characteristic of the Component, or that provides information about the Component that would be useful in the game.

○ Traits serve 3 purposes in Universalis.

1. They provide all players with a gauge of what the Component is like and how it should be used in the story.

2. They provide the Component with Importance. Importance is explained below, but basically, the more Coins that have been spent to buy Traits for a Component, the more

57

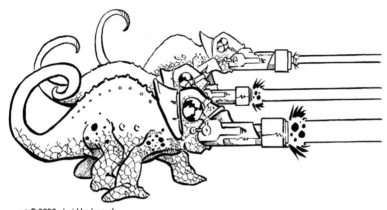

art © 2002, david hedgecock

Doom Cannons advancing on target, assault lasers blazing.

Important the Component is to the story, and the harder it is to remove from the story.

3. They can be Drawn upon to provide dice to roll in Complications.

○ The first Trait that is purchased for any Component should be its Role.

○ Adding one Trait to a Component costs 1 Coin.

○ A Component's Importance equals its number of Traits.

During the scene in the Slytheran Queen's throne room, Dave had Created the dreaded Doom Cannons for 1 Coin. That Coin bought the basic Trait *Doom Cannon* which defined the Role of the Component in the story. Later in the game, while the heroes are attempting to make their way back to the Meadow, Albert stages a Scene where he depicts the Slytheran army advancing slowly but inexorably towards Meadow. As part of the Scene, Albert decides to flesh out Doom Cannons since, as of yet, no one has any idea what they are.

Albert: Doom Cannons are actually *Chameleon Lizards*. They have *Thick Scaled Hides*, which have been

58

enhanced with *Armor Plating.* Being Chameleons, their *Eyes Can Swivel* in any direction. Since their normal means of feeding is to strike at range with their tongue with pinpoint accuracy, I'm giving them the Trait of *Pinpoint Accuracy.* But here's the thing. They've been surgically altered. Instead of tongues, they have a large-barreled assault laser cannon housed in their mouths (*Assault Laser Cannon for a Tongue* which he buys at x3 representing the power of the cannon). The Chameleons are controlled with a *Chip Embedded in their Brain.* When they go to strike a target with their tongues, it fires the laser instead.

[Albert pays 9 Coins for the above indicated Traits. Combined with the already purchased Role of Doom Cannon, the Component has an Importance of 10.]

DRAWING UPON TRAITS

Complications are described in Chapter 6, but essentially, the more dice you roll in a Complication, the more Bonus Coins you'll earn and the more likely you'll be to get to narrate first how the situation resolves. Your dice can come from one of two sources: you can either pay for them out of your own Wealth (1 Coin per die) or you can Draw Upon the Traits of Components that are participating in the Complication and which would be useful in that situation. Each applicable Trait allows one die to be added or subtracted from an appropriate Dice Pool for free.

It is likely that when the battle is engaged against these Doom Cannons, some player will narrate Meadow Troopers attempting to destroy them. Since it is likely that the Doom Cannon will be controlled by a different player than the player controlling the troopers, a Complication will result. In any Complication where the Doom Cannons are attempting to avoid being destroyed they have 2 relevant Traits *Thick Hides,* and *Armor Plating,* which can be Drawn upon to provide 2 dice to their Dice Pool in their defense. Unless, of course, the player Controlling the crafty troopers can come up with a means of damaging the lizards in which armor plating wouldn't help them (like drowning, perhaps).

59

BUYING THE SAME TRAIT MULTIPLE TIMES

A player can buy the same Trait multiple times for a Component. This can be done to indicate a particular advantage in that Trait. This can be recorded with a simple x2 or x3 (etc.) after the Trait name.

A multiple Trait allows multiple dice to be drawn during Complications. During narration, additional consideration should be given to the magnitude of the added advantage.

Also, the additional copies of the Trait provide additional Importance. If a player deemed it important enough to designate a character as being *Very Strong* by way of having a Trait of *Strong x2*, as opposed to simply defining the character as *Strong*, it is presumed that this additional strength will carry some impact for the story.

Similarly, a Trait of *Colossal Strength* provides the same one die for Complications that *Works out on Weekends* provides unless it is bought with a multiplier to reflect its greater magnitude. Without that, the difference will be in how the Trait is narrated and in what situations players allow it to be drawn upon for a die without Challenge.

If a player's primary goal is to get additional dice for use in a certain type of Complication, often times using Traits creatively can be more effective. Instead of buying *Sword Master x3*, consider buying *Sword Master, Incredible Reflexes* and *Combat Awareness* as three distinct Traits. All three are likely to be legitimate Traits to Draw Upon in a sword fight, but each has additional uses as well.

If, however, the character's concept truly demands an extraordinary caliber of sword mastery, the first option is perfectly acceptable.

ROLE

A Role is a standard Trait that every Component must have. It is the most basic form of defining "what the Component is and how it should be used." A Role is sufficient to bring the Component into existence.

Roles can be just about anything. For a character they could be a profession like *Accountant, Sheriff, Knight,* or *Scientist.* They could have a more story-related purpose like *Bully, Cynic, Troublemaker,* or even *Comic Relief.* They could have a Role based on their relationship to another Component like *Jeb's Son*

or *Dirk's Sidekick*. For a location, the Role is usually an actual place name or something descriptive about the place like *Dry Gulch, Abandoned Warehouse, Joe's House, Red's Bar & Grill*, or *Spooky Old Mansion*. For a prop, the Role typically defines what the prop is: a *Sword, Car, Gun,* or *Religion*.

Oftentimes, the Role involves multiple related Traits that could be purchased separately. For instance, the *Spooky Old Mansion* could be bought as a single Trait for 1 Coin; or it could be bought as *Mansion, Spooky,* and *Old,* for 3 Coins. The *Accountant* might be an *Accountant,* at *Myrex Corp* costing 2 Coins. The car might be a *Souped-up, Cherry-Red, Dodge Charger* costing 3 Coins. The deciding factors are how Important the player wants the Component to be and how many dice they'd like to be able to Draw Upon in Complications.

A Role coveys a basic set of characteristics that make the Component identifiable. For instance, a horse Created by paying 1 Coin for the Trait *Horse* will have four legs, hooves, eat hay and someone looking at it would say, "Hey, that's a horse." However, this horse has no particular ability, strength or speed. What this means is that while the horse exists in the world and can be included in the story and described as doing anything a horse would typically do (and is worth 1 Coin in Complications where being a horse would be an advantage), it is little more than scenery at this point.

How Roles are used in the game and how broadly they can be interpreted is often something best specified with a Tenet. For example, the above *Horse* is a horse. But, if a player tried to narrate a character riding it, would another player be justified in pointing out that no one had said the horse had been broken? Is it a riding horse, a war horse, a wild horse, a work horse, or a race horse? Play groups should decide for themselves how detailed they want to require Roles to be, or even if they would consider *War Horse* to be two separate Traits altogether (*Horse* and *Trained for War*). Since it is beyond the scope of any set of rules to account for a nearly infinite array of possible permutations, Universalis specifically leaves these decisions up to individual play group preference, either defined as a game Tenet or determined organically during play as described on page 45.

A Component with nothing defined but a single Role Trait is of limited Importance. A Role can be Drawn upon to provide one die during Complications in which that Role would be useful (or

61

one die per Trait that applies, if the Role consists of multiple Traits). For example, if the Complication involved the need to pull a wagon, one die can be drawn from the Role Trait *Work Horse,* as this is something that work horses are certainly useful for (of course, some groups may want to specify the difference between a pack horse, a cart horse, or a plow horse and may not be satisfied with *Work Horse* as being specific enough). Other Groups might decide that *Work* and *Horse* is actually 2 Traits. If they're paid for separately they can each be Drawn Upon for dice if appropriate.

PROPER NAME

The actual name of a Component is bought like any other Trait. Buying a proper name for a Component serves three purposes. First, it helps identify that Component as something special to be paid attention to. It is a staple of movies and literature that "named characters" are more important than "unnamed extras." Second, because it is an additional Trait, it does, in fact, increase the Component's Importance in game terms as well (see page 78 for more about Importance). Third, for a character only, a proper name Trait can be Drawn Upon to provide one die for any Complication of any type involving that character. Essentially, if characters are important enough to name, they should be guaranteed impact in a scene.

This does not apply to locations and props, simply because the relationship between in-game name and meta-game importance doesn't have a parallel in movies and literature. The heirloom gold watch so important to a character is simply *Grandfather's watch* - it isn't itself given a proper name. For props that would legitimately have a proper name, such as Excalibur, the name exists as a Trait that gives additional Importance, but is not normally something that can be Drawn Upon. Of course, for a prop (like Excalibur) that is itself an item of extraordinary stature, a Rules Gimmick can certainly be used to give the item proper name status.

Thus, in a barroom brawl, the character identified as simply the *Accountant* does not provide any dice because that Role does not convey any particular fighting ability. However, *John Oswald,* the *Accountant* does provide one die by virtue of being a named character. John's *Pocket Calculator* which he's named *Doris*, on the other hand, does not, because Doris is a prop and not a character, so the proper name rule doesn't apply.

> In the scene in the throne room, Bob took Control over *General #2* and gave him the proper name of *Frederich von Stuben.* As a named character in the game, Frederich is now able to contribute one die to any Complication he's involved with (Drawn from his name) just for being important enough to have been given a proper name in the story.

GROUP TRAITS

It is entirely possible for a Component to represent more than one item or person. This can be accomplished simply by adding a Group Trait to the Component indicating a specific or general number of members, such as adding *Three* to the Component *Gangsters*, or *Squad* to the Component *Riflemen.* The most common format, is to simply append the Group Trait to the Component Role making for *Three Gangsters* or *Squad of Riflemen.*

It is also common to purchase the Group Trait multiple times to represent increasingly larger groups. This may be a one-to-one ratio of additional members to additional Traits, but it doesn't need to be.

The additional Group Traits serve three functions:

○ To define a relative size of the group for purposes of aiding in player narration.

○ To draw additional dice from during a Complication in any situation where added numbers would be an advantage.

○ To provide additional Importance to the Component, making it more difficult to eliminate because of numbers.

If the Component is a fairly significant one, and each member is of sufficient stature, then each Group Trait could well represent a single member (if the Components are of very high significance, of course, each member could simply be entirely bought and paid for as a separate Component altogether). If, however, the Component is meant to be simply a throwaway opponent for the characters (like a squad of enemy troopers) or to represent very large numbers (like an army battalion, or a mob of sports fans), then the Group Trait can be left as an

63

abstraction of the actual numbers involved. Players can use the Challenge mechanic if they feel a given Group Trait doesn't reflect the numbers sufficiently.

Example Group Traits include *Team* of *Sled Dogs, Pair* of *Figure Skaters, Many Parked Cars, Crowd of Shoppers, Several Committee Members, Large Staff, etc.*

> For example, after defining the Doom Cannons, Albert decides that he doesn't know how many such war machines are in the Slytheran Army, but he decides that his Scene shows more than one for added dread. So he adds the Trait *Lance* to represent the unit size and then adds x3 to represent that a Lance of Cannon consists of several members. This costs an additional 3 Coins and brings the Importance of the Component to 13. Obviously, by spending so many Coins, Albert is saying that destroying these cannon should be a cornerstone of the scene (or scenes) depicting the battle between the Meadow People and the Slytheran.

RELATIONSHIP TRAITS

Traits can define relationships between Components. For instance: Super Villain Archon can have a Trait *Hates the Vindicator.* Princess Ridela can have a Trait *Thinks Sir Ulaf is a Crude Boor.* Lancelot can have the Traits *Loves Guenevere,* and *Loyal to Arthur.* These Traits not only provide additional Importance to the character (if the characters are worth defining relationships for, they must have some importance to the story), but also can be used to Draw Upon for dice in a Complication connected to that relationship. For instance, if Ulaf attempts to seduce Princess Ridela, the above Trait would likely be drawn upon by the player Controlling the princess to resist the attempt. If Guenevere were in danger, Lancelot might Draw Upon his love Trait to gain an additional die to try and save her.

Note that there are both definitional relationships and emotional relationships. Definitional relationships are those that identify an objective connection, but don't express feeling or opinion. These include Traits like *Spouse* or *Boss.* Since definitional relationships are typically a two-way street, a single Coin can buy the corresponding relationship for both Components. For example: a player buys a Trait for Jill of *Jack's Sister.* This

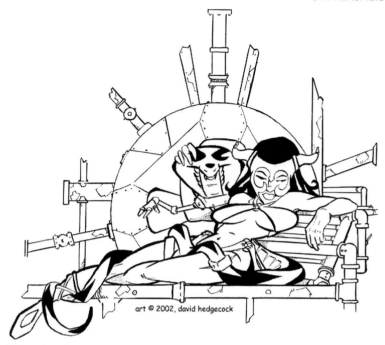

The traitor, Lady Alasandre, with the snake she uses to deliver intelligence to the Slytheran High Command.

art © 2002, david hedgecock

leads to the corollary Trait for Jack of *Jill's Brother*, which does not cost extra to record. Since emotions can be felt by one party but not the other, emotional relationships do not automatically generating a matching Trait in the other party. Those must be bought separately.

> In the throne room dialog scene, General von Stuben mentioned the strong defenses of the Meadow People. He knew of them because of the treacherous spy, Lady Alasandre, a self-styled Meadow aristocrat who has betrayed her people's secrets for promises of a position of power in the occupation government. As an added complication, Bob gave the lady a Trait of *Obsessive Lust for Turk Reigns* (all part of his apparent quest to see Turk suffer). Since this is an emotional relationship rather than a definitional one, it does not automatically spawn a corollary Trait in Turk, but can be used to provide dice in all sorts of interesting ways.

65

POSSESSION TRAITS

The most basic way to give someone a possession is simply to list it as a Trait of the owning Component. This is especially true of minor utilitarian items. For example, one of the Traits of a cowboy might be *Pair of Pearl-Handled Revolvers,* which could be Drawn Upon to provide dice in a Complication any time guns are used, or even in a social scene where the pearl handles might have some influence. Another character might have his *Pet Dog Fido* as a Trait, or *Sharp Pressed Suits,* or *Carries Lots of Cash,* etc.

Components that aren't characters can have possessions as well. A mansion can have *Lavish Furnishings.* A car can have *Fuzzy Dice.* A corporation can have an *Enormous Headquarters* and a *Sleek Company Jet.* A political party can have a *Staff of Volunteers.*

Possessions are treated just like any other Trait, except that they can be separated from their Component and become a new Component. This is, in fact, the essential definition of a Possession. If it can be separated from its Component and stand by itself as its own Component, it's a Possession.

○ Spend 1 Coin to remove a Possession from a Component and Create it as its own Component.

○ If the Possession consists of several words or phrases, select one to be the Role Trait of the new Component and pay 1 Coin each to convert the rest into Traits of that new Component.

For instance, *Enormous Headquarters* becomes *Headquarters* with the Trait of *Enormous* for 2 Coins. *Sharp Pressed Suits* can become *Suits* with the Traits of *Sharp-Looking* and *Well-Pressed* for 3 Coins.

> During the scene with the snapping turtle described on page 36, it was mentioned that the character Turk Reigns possesses an XR-27 Hyperblast Rifle as a Trait. This Trait was crossed off Turk's record sheet when the weapon was snapped in half by the hungry turtle, allowing Turk to escape death. This is an example of the simple type of possession.

OWNERSHIP TRAITS

Most Possessions will just be recorded as a Trait of the Component that owns them. Sometimes, however, the item is important enough to the story to be worth Creating as a separate Component of its own, like King Arthur's sword, Excalibur. When a Possession is its own Component, an Ownership Trait is used to indicate who the owner is. An Ownership Trait is a special kind of Relationship Trait. Since it's a definitional relationship, both sides can be added for the same Coin. For instance, buying the Trait *Owns Excalibur* for King Arthur automatically also adds *Owned by King Arthur* to Excalibur for free.

Excalibur could just be added as a Trait to King Arthur. It then could be split off to form its own Component separate from King Arthur for 1 Coin as described on page 66. The appropriate Ownership Traits are purchased automatically with that same Coin.

Any existing Component can become the property of any other existing Component simply by purchasing the appropriate Ownership Trait as long as it can be justified by the player's narrative. You are free to Challenge any attempt to assign ownership that doesn't make sense or that you just don't agree with. There is no limit on how many Components may be owned by a single owner.

There are several game mechanic effects that come as a result of this Trait.

○ If the owning Component is Introduced into a scene, the owned Component may be (if desired and appropriate) be automatically Introduced as well for free.

○ In most cases, a Coin can be spent by a player to separate the owned Component from its owner (if it is something which can be dropped or left behind, etc). This is akin to paying to remove Traits as described on page 82. It does, like all uses of Coins, have to be justified. It is not enough to simply spend the Coin and declare the item separated. Depending on Control this may require a Complication to accomplish. Otherwise the owned item can be eliminated from play by overcoming its own Importance.

○ If both the owner and Possession are present in the

scene, the player who is Controlling the owner also automatically Controls the Possession. If you Take Over the owner, you also automatically gain control of the Possession as well. If the Possession is separated from its owner or Introduced without its Owner it can be Controlled on its own.

○ The owner's Importance is increased by the Importance of all owned Possessions for as long as those Possessions remain owned. If the Components are separated, they lose this advantage. In other words if a 5 Importance character owns a 3 Importance item, the character is treated as if he has an Importance of 8 unless he is separated from the item.

The Ownership rule was specifically designed for "signature" possessions, like a mad scientist's gizmo, James Bond's gadgets, a Jedi's light saber, Thor's hammer, Arthur and Excalibur and other similar relationships. However, with a little judicious application, Possessions and the Ownership Trait can become a real story driver. A wealthy tycoon's assets can be defined as Possessions. Bringing the tycoon down can involve separating him from each of those assets. Similarly a major villain's body guards can be possessions. Their abilities add to their master's Importance, protecting him from defeat, until one by one, they themselves are defeated.

Important Note: It is not necessary for all of a character's belongings to be defined with Ownership Traits as separate Components using these rules. In fact, most often they won't be. Treat most ordinary props and items as simple Possession Traits as described above. Only if the item is some how extraordinary should it be Created as a separate Component and treated in this manner.

As an example: Kevin McCrae has been created as a member of the Meadow Team.. He is the team's technician and engineer. He also has as a pet skylar named Fritz. Ed, who Created Kevin as a character, also Created skylars as small winged lizard-like creatures about the size of a dragonfly, which eat fruit. As a bit of color (which didn't cost him anything except the 1 Coin for the name) Ed described how Kevin gave his pet a Slytheran name (remember Slytherans have been defined as having Prussian names) as a joke since it's a reptile.

Kevin McRae and his pet Skylar "Fritz."

Ed could have defined *Fritz* simply as a Trait for Kevin, but he became so enamored of the little guy that he Created him as a separate Component complete with Traits like *Skylar Pet* (Role), *Devoted to Kevin*, and *Highly Trained*, with an *Embedded Control Chip* and of course the name *Fritz*. Throughout play, the players agree that *Fritz* is enough of a character to benefit from the proper name rules. Kevin was then given the Possession Trait *Owns Fritz* for 1 Coin, which automatically adds *Owned by Kevin* to Fritz for that same Coin.

WORLD TRAITS

It is often convenient to think of the game world itself as an actual Component. Each individual scene can be thought of as its own separate Component as well. Players can purchase Facts explicitly for a scene or the world itself just like purchasing Traits for a Component.

For example: Facts related to the weather or time of day might

69

be bought for a scene. The laws of how magic works or what level of technology is available in the game might be bought as a Tenet for the world itself (or at least the part of it where play takes place).

> Early on in the game, in keeping with the Tenet Albert proposed about playing in a Science Fiction game and the Tenet Dave proposed about the use of animals, Ed introduced a Fact for the "game world."

> **Ed:** Both the Meadow People and the Slytheran use computer chips embedded in the brain to control their animals and make them do their bidding. [This costs 1 Coin for the Fact. Some play groups may prefer to treat this as two separate Facts, one for the Meadow People and one for the Slytheran and charge 2 Coins.]

MASTER AND SUB COMPONENTS

Master and Sub Components are an advanced way to leverage Component Creation in order to populate an entire world without breaking the bank.

One Component is defined as the Master Component, which defines the features held in common by an entire class or category. It costs 1 Coin to purchase the Trait *Master Component* which allows that Component to serve as a template for designing other (Sub) Components. A Master Component cannot have a proper name and should only possess Traits that can be considered typical of that entire class. They cannot be introduced into scenes or manipulated as distinct individuals. Master Components don't technically exist as an entity in the game. They simply define a template from which actual Components (Sub Components) can be designed.

A Sub Component is Created merely by buying a Trait for 1 Coin which defines the Component as being a member of the class defined by the Master Component. There is no limit to the number of Sub Components that can be tied to any single Master, nor is there a limit to the number of Master Components that a single Component can be tied to (save plausibility and the willingness of players to Challenge). Note that throughout these rules, all rules for Components apply to Sub Components, except as noted here.

70

There are several game mechanic effects that accompany the Master-Sub relationship.

1. The Sub Component is assumed to have all of the Traits of the Master Component without them having to be paid for individually. These Traits can be Drawn Upon during Complications. Multiple Sub Components can Draw Upon the same Master Component Trait during the same Complication, just as if each had that Trait themselves separately. For instance, the Master Component *Zombie* has *Feels No Pain* as a Trait. There are three individual characters in the scene all of whom have *Zombie* as a Trait identifying them as Sub Components. As a result, each has access to *Feels No Pain,* and in an appropriate Complication players can draw upon that Trait from each character to provide a die (three dice total, one from each zombie).

2. The Importance of the Sub Component is not increased by the Traits of the Master Component. Even though the Sub Components can use these Traits, they are not counted towards the Sub Component's own Importance. Thus, even though the Master Component *Zombie* itself has many Traits, allowing its individual Sub Components to Draw Upon many dice during Complications, a Sub Component whose only Trait is *Zombie #12* still has an Importance of only 1 and can be eliminated with a single Coin.

3. Sub Components can have their own individual Traits in addition to being members of the Master Component Class. These Traits are not shared by other Sub Components or the Master, and do count towards that Sub Component's Importance normally. For instance, one of the Zombies can be named *Fred* and given the Traits *Remembers Who He Was* and *Doesn't Like the Taste of Brains* to set him apart from the rest. This increases his own Importance by 3 but doesn't affect the rest of the horde. They'd have to buy their own.

4. It is possible for the Sub Component to have a Trait that effectively negates a Trait provided by the Master Component. Such a Trait prevents the Sub Component from Drawing on that Trait of the Master Component and adds to the Sub Component's Importance. It is, after all, increasing that Sub Component's individuality and thus Importance to the story. For instance:

71

one of many Traits ascribed to the Master Component *Zombie* is *Slow Shambling Gait,* a negative Trait that is usually Drawn Upon against them. A particular character who has the Trait *Zombie* (and is hence a Sub Component of the Zombie Class), also has the Trait *Doesn't Have a Slow Shambling Gait.* This Trait increases the Importance of that character while at the same time preventing a player from Drawing Upon the *Slow* Trait. They effectively negate each other.

> **DESIGN NOTE: WHY DOES IT ALWAYS HAVE TO BE ZOMBIES?**
>
> After dozens of demo games and actual play reports from hundreds of players over the last few years, one genre element keeps cropping up more often then any other – Zombies. We've had western zombies, ninja zombies, zombies in space, zombies at summer camp and even a Zombie Elvis. For whatever reason, the shambling dead have proven an easy well to go to for ideas.
>
> So this section is dedicated to all of those players who just ain't happy unless their games include lurching corpses wailing for "brains..."

5. A Component may be a Sub Component of more than one class. For instance, Fred the Zombie may also have the Trait *Policeman* as a Sub Component and have all of the Traits that have been attributed to the *Policeman* Master Component as well.

6. The Master Component's own Importance is increased by the Importance of all of its Sub Component members. Thus, the only way to wipe out all of the zombies from the world, would be to first Eliminate all of the individual zombie characters in the story, and then Eliminate the Master Component itself.

> In our sample game, Bob Created Slytheran Shock Troopers as a Master Component. He gave them the following Traits: *Slytheran Shock Trooper* (as a Role), *Acute Viper-like Sensing Pits, Venomous Fangs, Fierce Fighters, Single-Mindedly Aggressive,* and *Blindly Loyal.* He equipped them with a *High-Power Assault Rifle* and

art © 2002, david hedgecock

A Slytheran Shock Trooper with body armor and assault rifle.

73

Body Armor. This cost 9 Coins, including the one designating this as a *Master Component*.

From now on individual Shock Troopers can be Introduced into the scene for a single Coin (to purchase the Sub Component Trait *Slytheran Shock Trooper*. Each trooper will have access to all of the above Traits of the Master Component, but itself will have only an Importance of 1 (allowing our heroes to kill them by the dozen as required).

Additionally, using the Group Trait rules, a Component can be Created called *Slytheran Shock Troopers, Shock Squad x3*. This would cost 4 Coins and have an Importance of 4. It would be a Sub Component of the Slytheran Shock Trooper and represent an entire squad of such troops in a single Component.

EXTENDED EXAMPLE OF CREATING COMPONENTS

When Dave Framed the very first scene of the game, he provided an initial direction for the entire story:

Dave: Ok, let's get started. The place is the *Town* of *Meadow* [This costs 2 Coins and Creates a Component with *Town* as its Role and *Meadow* as a proper name. The same Coin that defined the Role, also establishes the Component as the location for the upcoming scene.]

Since we've decided that the characters are all diminutive little people, we'll assume that everything is appropriately scaled in miniature unless otherwise noted with a Trait. [Here Dave is proposing a Rules Gimmick so that every Component he Creates doesn't have to have *Miniature in Size* as a Trait. This costs 1 Coin.]

We see the town from above, like from a bird flying overhead [This is pure color, Dave is just giving screen direction type information in order to better paint a picture for his fellow players. This costs nothing.]

It is a *quiet little community* of *small cottages* and *red tile roofs*. Set in *The Middle of a Small Meadow*,

the town is *Surrounded by Grasses Taller than the Buildings* and *Bright Wildflowers Towering Like Trees*. [As per his Gimmick, Dave is noting that the grasses and flowers are normal sized not miniature.]

Throughout the town are signs of contrast: here are *Streets Paved with Pebbles like Cobblestones* and an *Old Fashioned Wind Mill*. There is a *Satellite Dish* and *Antennae for Cell Phones*. [As Dave is speaking, he holds a handful of Coins from his Wealth. When he mentions something that sounds to him like its worth paying for, he drops a Coin into the Bank. Albert, who is serving as the Recorder for the group, scribbles furiously each time. The players are using the simple expedient when defining Traits that if it's something you want written down for future reference, it costs you a Coin. The above Traits (indicated in italics) cost Dave 10 Coins. Including the 2 spent initially, Meadow now has an Importance of 12. Add in the Rules Gimmick and Dave has spent 13 of his initial Coins, but has really put his stamp on the story by giving substance to the somewhat vague Tenets the group came up with.]

It is *Early Summer* and the flowers are in bloom. *Oak and Beech Trees Surround the Meadow* and are just starting to take on a deeper shade of green. They dominate the horizon like mountains. [Here Dave has set the time for the scene. Since this is the first scene of the game, Dave has used an actual calendar reference. Most other scenes' time will be set in relative terms (referring to how long before or after a previous scene it was). Any scene set immediately following the previous one costs nothing, but since there has been no previous scene, this costs 1 Coin (a fair price, since Dave has now established a season for the story to start in). Dave doesn't pay for the flowers being in bloom. He decides that that is just color as is the green of the trees and no other player feels differently enough to Challenge him on it. He does drop a Coin on *Oak and Beech Trees*

75

Surround the Meadow to make that a Trait for the town. Given that the town is in a meadow, one could assume the trees as a given, but Dave feels like making it explicit and getting to decide what kind of trees they are in the bargain. Albert, keeping record, tacks on *...like mountains* to the end of the Trait for free, feeling that that is all part of same Trait and Dave has spent plenty of Coins (15) so far anyway.]

Down in the *Square* there are three figures standing about like they're waiting for something. That's the end of my turn. [Dave buys yet another Trait for the town, ensuring that it has a proper *Square* and bringing the total Importance of Meadow to 14 so far. He then pays 4 more Coins, 1 each for the three figures, and 1 Coin for the activity of them waiting for something. Ordinarily the Coins to Create those figures would entitle Dave to define a Role for each of them. However, Dave is instead doing something unusual (unusual enough that some groups may require a Rules Gimmick to allow it). He has paid for the figures, but left defining their Role up to someone else. This is Dave's way of getting another player to kick-start the story. He set the stage, he Introduced three potential characters, and now he's leaving defining those characters and what they are doing to someone else. Dave's turn ends (having spent 20 Coins on Framing the Scene). Play passes to Ed.]

Ed has his own ideas about what he wants the story to be about. Dave's initial setting has changed them somewhat (Ed was planning on the setting being more urban industro-tech and less European rural-quaint), but in a more important way, it dovetails nicely. Ed is planning on having the character's homes threatened by an enemy, and Dave has nicely created that home.

Ed: Ok, the camera zooms in on one of the buildings *On the Square*. It is an *Imposing Stone Edifice* with the words *Defense Command Headquarters* carved above the door. We watch as the three figures walk inside. [Ed has created DefCom HQ as a

A SUITABLE NUMBER OF TRAITS

Both the example of the Doom Cannons on page 58 and the Slytheran Shock Trooper found on page 72 feature a fairly significant number of Traits (13 and 9 respectively). This is largely to illustrate the wide range and variety of items that could be considered Traits during a game. The actual number of Traits that any given Component should have is entirely up to your individual play group to decide. You may elect to set some parameters formally as a Tenet or the amount may just arise organically during play. The correct amount is purely a matter of group preference.

It is highly recommended, however, to make sure that the Components are appropriately scaled with each other in a given story. If the common enemy grunt Shock Troopers, meant to be cut down by the dozen, are going to be given access to 9 Coins to Draw on in a Complication, then the story's heroes had best have a sufficient number of Coins to Draw on themselves. On the other hand, if the protagonists have only a small handful of Traits, then minor thugs and opponents may often have nothing other than a single Role Trait.

new location for 3 Coins, and spent 1 Coin on the actions of the as yet mysterious figures. The carving of the name above the door Ed leaves as color.]

Ok, I'm changing the location. We are now in the *Office of General Jackson Trudeau* which is *Inside DefCom HQ.* [This costs 2 Coins and Creates the offices as a Component which will serve as the new location for the scene. After a moment's discussion, Albert records *Inside DefCom HQ* as an Ownership Trait indicating the Offices are "owned" by the building. The corollary Trait of *Contains General Trudeau's Office* is added to DefCom HQ for free. This is a creative way to connect locations together. Albert goes back and treats the *On the Square* Trait the same way making DefCom HQ a Possession of the Town.]

The General is present, as are the three unknown

figures. [Since the location has been changed, existing Components from the old location are assumed to automatically change location without having to be paid for. Ed pays 2 Coins to Create the character of the General (his Role) and define his proper name.]

The General's Offices are *Spartan* and *Meticulous* [These are Traits added to the location for 1 Coin each. The General's Office now has an Importance of 4. DefCom HQ has an Importance of 3 plus the additional 4 for "owning" the office for a total of 7. As noted above Meadow has an Importance of 14 but since it "owns" Defense Command Headquarter its Importance is increased by 7 to 21. Ed is planning to drive the story towards a threat to Meadow and between himself and Dave has ensured that it will take any would-be enemy 21 Coins (so far) to destroy the town.]

At this point, the scene continues. Ed establishes his potential threat — an old enemy which he names the Slytheran. Christine Takes Control of one of the figures and on her turn begins defining the character of Marissa. The other characters will eventually become Kevin and Turk and the players go on to establish them as a team ordered by General Trudeau to investigate Slytheran activity across the river. The story has now been given a direction.

INJURING, DAMAGING, & ELIMINATING COMPONENTS

IMPORTANCE

Importance is a measure of how valuable a particular Component is to the story. It is assumed that the more time and effort (and Coins) that have been spent describing a Component, the more valuable it is, and thus the more difficult it should be to remove from the story. A Component that has been Created with few Traits beyond a Role (like *Thug #3*) is assumed to not be very important to the story and thus can be removed easily. Or to put it another way, while the army of thugs may, in fact, be an important element in the story, no one thug has any value on

78

his own...unless that thug is individualized further by purchasing additional Traits.

○ **Importance equals 1 for every Trait the Component has.**

Marissa Tournou is one of the main characters in this game. She was Created by Christine and throughout the game has accumulated the following Traits: *Marissa Tournou* (proper name), *Trained Killer x2* (Role, which she's particularly good at), *Physically Rugged, Fiercely Determined, Command Ability, Impatient, Hard Cold Demeanor* and has as Possessions a *Flame Retardant Jump Suit, IR Goggles,* and a *Type VII Laser Pistol.* All told this is a total of 11 Traits which cost 11 Coins and provides Marissa with an Importance of 11. Later in the story it's also revealed that she had a *Torrid Affair with Jerek* and *Feels Betrayed by Jerek* which ups her Importance to 13.

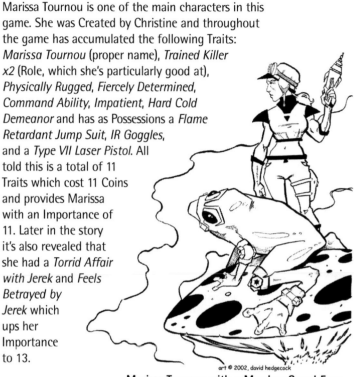

art © 2002, david hedgecock

Marissa Tournou with a Meadow Guard Frog standing watch atop a toadstool sentry tower.

ELIMINATING A COMPONENT

A Component can be Eliminated for many reasons: a character can get killed, a location or prop can get destroyed, an organization can get disbanded, etc. In order to do this a player must spend a number of Coins equal to the Component's Importance. For instance: *Jack,* the *Alcoholic, Bartender* has three Traits and thus an Importance of 3. During a gangland attack on the bar, a player wants poor Jack to get whacked. 3 Coins will do the job. Kang the Merciless, Imperial overlord of the Dark Empire, has a couple of dozen Traits and many Possessions. It will take far more Coins to Eliminate Kang. Of course to do this the player

79

will have to either Control the Component or else engage it in a Complication.

Players can feel free to narrate any variety of colorful effects (subject to Challenge, of course) to describe how the Component is eliminated. Each Coin spent on the Elimination serves as a Fact that can be narrated to describe the details of how it was done. For instance Jack the hapless Bartender was *accidentally caught in the crossfire, riddled with bullets*, and wound up *slumped across the bar* as the result of the 3 Coins spent to Eliminate him. These are not added as Traits to Jack but rather serve as Facts to establish exactly how Jack died if that should later become important to know.

The game mechanic effect of Eliminating a Component is to render the Component unavailable to be Introduced into scenes chronologically set in the future. The Component could still be introduced into scenes set in the past (before it was Eliminated). However, while additional Traits may be bought for the Component in those prior scenes, they will not (simply by increasing the Component's Importance) override the fact that the Component has been Eliminated. In other words, if, in a subsequent scene, a player flashes back to Jack the Bartender and adds the Traits of *College Graduate*, and *Has a Young Son*, Jack's Importance has been increased to 5. That does not change the fact that Jack was killed during the hit even though the player spent only 3 Coins instead of 5 to do it. In stories, it is often the case that a character becomes more important after he is dead.

What Elimination actually represents is left to the player to decide. Like any expenditure of Coins, Coins spent to overcome Importance must be justified. Elimination often represents the death of a character or the destruction of a location or prop. However, it does not have to mean this. It could mean anything that renders the Component out of play for the rest of the story. In the case of particularly minor Components, the cause of their Elimination might be left unstated. The faceless mook is simply put down. No one really cares if he lives or dies. The empty gun is merely cast aside never to be seen again in the story. The stolen car is abandoned, the key witness disappears overseas, The character takes an extended vacation. Whatever the reason is, the Component is now effectively out of the rest of the story.

Unless... (of course there is an "unless"). Certain genres practically require the return of a villain long thought defeated, or the

80

return of a loved one who wasn't dead after all – they just had amnesia for ten years. The broken sword can be forged anew, and the One Ring lost for generations can be rediscovered.

To "resurrect" a Component in this way, a player must merely spend a number of Coins equal to its current Importance (which may have been increased since it was first Eliminated). If this is done in a plausible enough manner to avoid (or overcome) Challenge from other players, then that Component can be welcomed back to the land of the living. In fact, Eliminating a Component may be used as a way of preventing a character's death. If a player pays Coins equal to the Importance of the Arch Villain, he could narrate how the villain manages to escape into another dimension, thereby preventing another player from paying that many Coins to narrate his capture and execution. Either way the villain is out of the story and no longer plaguing mankind...for now.

> During the final battle for the Meadow, the team is at last confronted with the terrible Doom Cannons. The confrontation is handled as a Complication Originated by Dave, using the 13 point *Lance* x3 of *Doom Cannons* Albert had Created earlier.
>
> Following the resolution of the encounter, the players Controlling the heroes use the Bonus Coins earned in the Complication to narrate the defeat of the Doom Cannons. They can describe blasts of laser fire, fierce hand-to-hand combat, and feats of derring-do as desired. The Doom Cannon can be killed, driven off, taken prisoner, deactivated, or any other outcome the players desire that essentially equates to their defeat as a *Lance of Doom Cannons*. Since the lance has an Importance of 13, it requires 13 Coins to accomplish this. Using 13 Coins in this manner also entitles the players up to 13 Facts related to the Elimination of the Lance, and as much colorful description as desired (within reason, where "unreasonable" is defined by the other players' willingness to Challenge).

DAMAGING TRAITS

Coins can also be spent to damage or injure Components without having to first overcome their Importance. First, the Event

THE DEAD TRAIT

Virtually any concept can be added to a Component as a Trait. Inevitably players hit upon the idea of adding the Trait *Dead* to characters as a way of killing them more cheaply than buying off their Importance.

The difference is that Eliminating a character makes it so that character can not be Introduced into any future scenes. Simply adding *Dead* as a Trait does not. That character could still be Introduced into a scene and still have its Traits Drawn Upon in Complications. 1 Coin would be sufficient to remove the Trait and effectively "resurrect" the character again. Players could even narrate the character getting up and walking around and other players would have to Challenge them (backed by the weight of Fact) to prevent this.

For this reason players should only use Traits like *Dead* and its many variations (like *Destroyed* for non character Components) if playing a genre where characters can still actively influence the story even after they're dead. Stories featuring zombies, ghosts or Jedi come to mind. A more art house variation would be to phrase the narration of the dead character's activities such that it is the memory of the departed and the impact they had while alive that is actively influencing the story rather than the deceased themselves.

At other times, players should Eliminate a Component by paying Coins equal to its Importance if they want to kill or destroy it.

causing the injury must be paid for, then the effects of the injury or damage can be purchased. Damage and Injury can be handled in one of three ways.

1. Existing Traits can be Removed for 1 Coin each. If the character has a *.44 Magnum* as a Trait, it is a simple matter to cross that Trait off for 1 Coin. Instant disarmament. If the character has *Excellent Physical Condition* as a Trait, it is a simple matter to cross that Trait off as a result of suffering a debilitating illness.

2. New Traits can be purchased that reflect the nature of the damage. These Traits can then be Drawn Upon just like any other, albeit usually in a way detrimental to the Component suffering from them. A character may

CHAPTER 5: CREATING COMPONENTS

suffer from a *Broken Leg*, a car from a *Blown Tire*, a location from *Broken Windows* and *Smashed Furniture*.

Note that adding Traits in this manner actually increases a Component's Importance even though they represent injury. There are two principles at work here. First, the author of a story usually only takes the time to describe the injuries of characters who are important, thus a character's Importance in the game is increased when players do this. Second, in many stories the heroes take beating after beating but actually become more and more difficult to kill. In Universalis this is no surprise, as their Importance is going up every time they get a black eye.

The effect of such injury Traits in game terms is threefold: First, players should take the injury into account when narrating the Component's activities, possibly paying extra Coins to describe how it overcomes or avoids the handicap. Second, the injuries serve as a Fact in any Challenge against a player who's not taking the injury into account to another player's satisfaction. Third, in Complications where the injury or damage might have an effect, those Traits may be Drawn upon to reduce the Component's dice or add dice to an opponent to represent their impact.

3. If the player is actually Eliminating a Component, and is merely using the expenditure of the required Coins to graphically describe how this is accomplished, then the Coins are not buying additional injury Traits as in #2 above, they are just flavorful narration. For instance, a villain's henchman has an Importance of 5. A player is having the hero defeat and kill this henchman and has spent 5 Coins to do so. He describes a hard kick to the leg blowing out the knee, a twist to the arm dislocating the shoulder, and finally a chop to the throat crushing the larynx. These three injuries are not added as Traits to the henchman, they are just part of how the henchman was killed. If the henchman was not killed, then they would be added, and the henchman would now have an Importance of 8.

In the snapping turtle scene on page 36 we saw how Turk Reigns' *X-27 Hyperblast Rifle* Trait was Removed from the character record as a consequence of escaping with his life.

83

In the fight with the Doom Cannon, let's go back and assume the heroes only earned (or desired to spend) 5 Coins from the Complication. 5 Coins would not be enough to Eliminate the lance as a Component. Instead, the players could use the 5 Coins to damage the Component. First they Remove the *Chip Embedded in their Brain* Trait for 1 Coin to make the beasts harder for the Slytheran to manage. Then they weaken the *Assault Laser x3* by spending 2 Coins to reduce the Trait to x1. Then they reduce the *Lance x3* by 1 to *Lance x2* for 1 Coin representing how the team managed to actual fell one of the armored lizards. Finally, with the last Coin they add a new Trait *Slowed*. While this actually increases the Cannon's Importance it also provides a die in future Complication that the Meadow team players can use against the Doom Cannon. All told, the Doom Cannon Component now has an Importance of 10 instead of 13 which will make it slightly cheaper to Eliminate later on.

During Complications, both the winning and losing side will receive Bonus Coins. Assuming that the heroes were the winning side in the Complication with the Doom Cannon, the player Controlling the Cannon (Dave, the Originator of the Complication) would also have Bonus Coins to spend. In our example we'll assume he has 2 Bonus Coins. He wishes to spend them to give Marissa an injury from the battle. He describes how in the fight her leg was hit by blaster fire and now she has a *Severe Blaster Burn to the Leg x2* Trait (he essentially bought the same wound twice to demonstrate its severity). This injury serves to increase Marissa's Importance by 2 from 13 to 15 (until the wound is healed), but clearly her ability to walk has been compromised.

RESTORING TRAITS: HEALING, REPAIR, OR RECOVERY

Healing or repair of such damage and injury is simply handled by either paying to remove a damage or injury Trait which has been purchased (the *Broken Leg* heals), or paying to restore a Trait that had previously been removed (the character recovers from the illness and gets his *Excellent Physical Condition* back). In the case of a lost item, a Coin can be spent to have the item found, returning the Trait to the Character sheet.

> When Turk gets back to the Meadow, he almost certainly will requisition a new firearm from supply. The player Controlling Turk at the time can pay 1 Coin for the action and Restore the *X-27 Hyperblast Rifle* to the character record. Alternatively, the player may decide that Turk takes the opportunity to upgrade to the new X-30 model with the under-barrel grenade launcher, paying 2 Coins, one for the rifle and one for the launcher, essentially buying two new Traits instead of Restoring the old one.

> In a scene following the fight with the Doom Cannon, Christine decides to address Marissa's injury. She could simply spend 2 Coins to Restore both of the *Blaster Burn Traits*, justifying the expenditure by narrating some form of medical treatment. Instead, however, she proposes a Rules Gimmick for 1 Coin. Justified by Marissa's Trait of *Fiercely Determined* Christine proposes that Marissa is able to completely ignore (as if she didn't have the Trait at all) the injury to her leg until she gets full medical attention, however in return (to make the Gimmick less likely to be Challenged, and because she thinks it would be cool) she proposes that due to the added strain of pushing herself too hard and not caring for the injury properly, Marissa will acquire a *Slight Limp in Right Leg* Trait after the battle is over. That is, instead of paying 2 Coins to remove the 2 injury Traits entirely, Christine will pay 1 Coin to temporarily remove the 2 injury Traits and replace them later with a single permanent Trait; a war injury to be proud of. The rest of the players agree to this unusual way of dealing with an injury and so it becomes accepted as a rule.

USING TRAITS AS CONSTRAINTS ON PLAY

Traits are an extremely powerful tool for directing the story in a desired direction. Far more subtle than Challenges or Complications, Traits enable players to have a permanent ongoing effect on the game for a single Coin. For the rest of the game (unless the Trait is damaged or the Component is Eliminated), other players will have to take them into account during their narrations, or else risk having them used against them in a Challenge.

In Universalis, players have the authority to take the game in any direction they want by spending Coins. A key feature of the game is that the other players also have this ability, which means they may take the game in a direction different from your own. The tension between these different directions can yield some powerful and entertaining creative synergies, but it is often desirable to give the game some additional structure so that even though the whole story won't necessarily go in the direction you initially wanted, the important highlights can be included.

Traits provide the structure to the story. Build a network of relationships with your characters: who hates who and why, who is loyal, who is eager to please, who leads, and who follows. Give the characters a set of personality Traits that establishes behavior parameters: who is devious, who is honest, who is secretly jealous, who harbors an old resentment, who is gullible, who has trouble controlling their temper, and who consults a psychic before making tough decisions.

Go a step further and actually record goals and objectives. What does the character want? What is the character willing or not willing to do to get it? For instance "More than anything, Stacy wants money; she's willing to betray her husband, lie to her family, cheat her employer, but she would never do anything to hurt her son." Depending on your play group, the above may be anywhere from two to five distinct Traits. By defining these as Traits you've not only solidified your vision of the character for the other players (who most often will be more than happy to work with your directorial cues) but you've also got a solid foundation for Challenging players who try to take the character somewhere you'd rather not go.

If you find someone doing something with a character or other Component that seems radically different from what you had in mind, take a look at the list of Traits you gave it. Did you provide enough Traits to give the other players a sense of what you'd been thinking? When another player turns your dynamic femme fatale into a sad subservient doormat, check the Traits. Is there anything there that the other player's description is contradicting that you can use to bolster a Challenge? If not, there probably should have been. If you haven't spent Coins on it...it isn't true.

GAME PLAY NOTE: THE EFFECTIVE USE OF TRAITS

Contributed by Tony Irwin

What we came up with was that Traits should be viewed not just as situational modifiers (either giving or removing a die), but that clever selection of Traits can be used to enforce story logic. The thing about Facts is that they're very obviously control mechanisms for your vision of the story. As soon as you introduce one, everyone starts thinking "How will this affect me and my interests?"

I'm going to share a really sneaky secret. Bid ten Coins to get to Frame the Scene. Use however many Coins you need to get the basic structure in place. Then use the rest of those Coins to create Facts that complement and supplement each other. No one can Interrupt while you're Framing the scene until you've narrated an Event. Another time to do this is after winning a Complication when you get your uninterrupted opportunity to spend the Coins you won. Because your Facts supplement each other, if someone later spends a Coin to eliminate one of them, you've got others already in place to use to Challenge them doing that.

Facts really changed the way I look at Complications. Previously I'd be going into a Complication thinking "How many Coins can I win and keep for my little bank?" Now I actually think in terms of "Exactly how many Coins do I need to win in order to get the Facts I want into the game?" Same goes for framing scenes. I've played lots of games where no one was bothered about who framed the scene. If you didn't have anything you especially wanted do then the default bid was 0, because we figured "If I need to I can just take Control." Now, however, I and a couple of friends have twigged that framing a scene is actually the most powerful phase of the game in terms of getting your ideas into play.

Traits are a great way of clarifying "This is what I want the story to be about, and as an equal partner in this game I'm willing to commit myself this much in Coins to seeing it go this way." We do create great stories and have a wonderful time doing so! Honest!"

CHAPTER 6: COMPLICATIONS

○ Complications occur in one of two ways:
1. Whenever a player attempts to have a Component they Control do something to or with a Component they do not Control; or
2. When another player wishes to turn an Event into an Obstacle and purchases dice representing difficulty.
○ Resolving Complications involves players rolling dice against each other to see who gets the privilege of deciding the outcome.

COMPLICATION BASICS

1. Start a Dice Pool for each player who Controls a Component that is involved in the Complication. Align the Pools into opposing sides.
2. Players take turns around the table adding dice (d10s) to Pools (primarily their own) by Drawing upon Traits or buying dice with Coins.
3. When no one wishes to add any further dice, roll.
4. Count the number of dice that came up 1-5 in each Pool (a Success). The side with more Successes wins.
5. Players with Pools on the winning side get Bonus Coins equal to the total sum showing on their successful dice.
6. Players with Pools on the losing side get Bonus Coins equal to the number of dice rolled in their Pool.
7. The winning players, in order of most to least Coins received, use Coins to narrate Events and add, remove, or restore Traits as desired to any Component regardless of Control.
8. The winning player may use Coins to cancel Coins received by the losers.
9. Losing players, in order of most to least Coins received, do likewise (to any Component regardless of Control), limited by what has already been narrated.
10. Players do not have to spend all Coins received. Coins not spent can be kept and added to Wealth.

Complications are the core driving force in Universalis. You will not achieve the full potential of the game unless you are making effective use of Complications and looking for opportunities to drive your game to the next one. Mechanically, Complications are vital to the in-game economy because they provide the primary means of regenerating player Wealth. More than that, however, Complications are what keep the game from being an elaborate version of "pass the conch." More than just players sitting around a table taking turns making up stories, Complications force players to decide what is really important to them and serve as a springboard for inspiration.

Players will find that Complications are the reason it's so important to define the right Traits for the Components in the story. If you have a certain direction you want the story to go, make sure that the key characters are equipped to take events in that direction by giving them the Traits they need to get there. Those Traits will allow you to win Complications which will provide you with the Coins you need to narrate your desired outcome. More importantly, those Traits will allow other players to win Complications and earn Coins too. But in order to use them they will have to stay within the boundaries set by those Traits. In other words, in order to take advantage of the free Coins Traits can provide during Complications, players will voluntarily choose to stay within the parameters you set with those Traits; assuming you defined them effectively.

Purchasing Traits becomes an investment in the future of the game. Traits cost 1 Coin, but can provide one die in Complications again and again. Those dice will then be converted back into Coins when they are rolled. Thus, you can acquire more Coins at any point in the game simply by starting a Complication and using the Traits already in place to provide dice. This will earn you free Coins even if you lose. By creating Components whose interests (skillfully defined by Traits) are naturally in conflict it becomes easy to find opportunities to Originate Complications.

Complications are competitions between players to determine who gets the first opportunity to narrate a resolution to a conflict between Components. Components are arrayed on opposing sides with their respective interests being represented by the players who Control them.

89

Complications arise when a player narrates a Component they Control taking action towards or against a Component

ON THE IMPORTANCE OF COMPLICATIONS

Contributed by Arturo González-Escribano.

For the first time I clearly noticed how important Complications are to my investment in the game. There was a moment where I had spent almost all my Coins in a scene. For the rest of the scene and even into the next one I did not have enough Coins to interrupt as many times as I wanted to. The story began to go in a way I didn't like so much, and I began to lose interest.

A Complication later and I had some control again. It took some time to figure out how to incorporate my ideas to their previous stuff, but as it began to take form I was rising up, highly interested, immediately.

It's nice how you can see this flow during the game.

they do not Control. The player narrating the action is deemed the Originator of the Complication and any Components used towards accomplishing the Originator's aims form the Source's side in the Complication. The Component or Components being affected or acted against by the Source Components are the Targets and they form the Target's side.

Alternatively, any player can, in the midst of another player's narration, initiate a Complication directly by purchasing dice representing an obstacle to that narration. These dice become the Source's side. The Target side will be whichever Components are impacted by the obstacle.

Any player who Controls a Component that is part of either side will build a Pool of dice to support that side. These Pools will be built by Drawing Upon appropriate Traits. Each Trait can add one die to a Pool that the Trait is deemed to benefit, or subtract one die from a Pool that it could be deemed to harm. Dice can also be purchased directly with Coins and added or subtracted from any Pool consistent with the narration accompanying their purchase.

Starting with the player who Originated the Complication and continuing with the normal rules for turn order and Interruption, players will have the opportunity to Draw Upon Traits from any Component present (including those they do not Control). They do this by narrating how a particular Trait applies to the given situation (either for or against a given Pool) and thereby claiming the Trait's die for that Trait for that Pool (either adding or subtracting). They may also use their narration to justify purchasing dice for 1 Coin each.

Once players have claimed all the Traits they desire and are done adding to the Pools, the dice are rolled. Any die that rolls 1-5 is considered to be a Success and the side which rolled the most Successes across all of its Pools is the winner.

Each player who had a Dice Pool on the winning side earns a number of Bonus Coins equal to the sum total on all of the successful dice rolled in their Pool. They then go in order of most Bonus Coins earned to least and spend those Coins to resolve the Complication.

Each player who had a Dice Pool on the losing side earns a number of Bonus Coins equal to the number of dice rolled in their Pool. They then go in order (after the last of the winning players has gone) of most Bonus Coins earned to least and spend those Coins on the final details of the Complication (as long as they don't contradict anything already narrated by the Winners).

Any Coins a player doesn't use can be added to their Wealth.

NEW CONCEPTS

ORIGINATOR

The player who started the Complication by interacting with a Component Controlled by another player; or who purchased dice to serve as an Obstacle during another player's narration, is the Originator of the complication. The Originator will build a Dice Pool on behalf of the Source of the Complication.

TARGET

The Components that the Originator is attempting to manipulate, affect, or interact with, as part of the Complication, are the Targets of the Complication. Any player who Controls a Targeted Component is a Target player and builds a Dice Pool on behalf of the Targets they Control.

Note: if the player who controls the Target is the same player as the Originator, there is no Complication. That player can simply manipulate, affect, or interact with those Components as desired as part of a normal turn. If that player really desires to turn the situation into a Complication they can ask other players to voluntarily Take Control of the desired Target Components and serve as the opposition in the Complication.

THE DICE POOLS

Each player who Controls an involved Component will have either a Source Dice Pool or a Target Dice Pool in the Complication. The Originator, by definition, will always have the first Source Dice Pool. Other players may also join the Source side if they Control Components whose interests they feel would be aligned with the Source, but not if they Control Components

> ### CREATIVE SOURCES OF DICE
> On your turn, or by Interrupting, you can increase your options.
> 1. Introduce a new Component into the scene and Draw Upon its Traits.
> 2. Purchase new Traits for an existing Component and then Draw Upon them.
> 3. Create a new Component, and purchase new Traits to Draw Upon.

that have already been identified by the Originator as Targets. Players may not have both a Source and a Target Dice Pool participating in the same Complication. If you already have a Dice Pool for one side you cannot start a Dice Pool for the other side, even if you Control Components that would seem to support that other side. Another player who is (or wishes to be) aligned with the other side can Take Over that Component from you in order to commit it to that other side.

All of the Dice Pools of a given side will be rolled and narrated independently by their players, but they are treated collectively for purposes of tallying Successes and determining the winning side.

During the Complication, players will add dice to their Pools by Drawing Upon Traits or purchasing them with Coins. In general, the Originator will be adding dice to their own Source Pool describing the nature of the threat, challenge, opponent, or obstacle. Target Pool players will be adding dice to their own Target Pool describing how the Target is trying to defeat, overcome, circumvent, or otherwise prevent the Originator's intended action from coming to pass.

Players without Pools of their own (because they don't Control any Source or Target Components) may participate as they choose by adding dice to any other player's Pool they have a desire to see prevail. If they have Control of a Component that is not yet involved in the Complication they can declare it in support of either the Target Side or Source Side (if they spend Coins to narrate an appropriate course of action that would get the Component involved) and start a Pool of their own accordingly.

Any player may also, on their turn (normally or by Interrupt), Introduce additional Components or Take Over non-committed Components and involve them in the Complication.

BUILDING THE DICE POOLS

After Originating a Complication, the players continue with their turns normally. Play passes around the table and players can Interrupt to take their turns according to all of the standard rules. The only exception is that the scene cannot be ended until the Complication is resolved. The Complication remains open so long as any player has an interest in it being open.

When narrating Events on your turns, you must keep in mind the nature of the open Complication. That Complication will likely be the dominant feature of the scene until it is resolved, and your narrations must: 1) take the existence of the Complication into account and 2) not narrate any Events that assume the Complication resolves in a particular fashion.

In addition to the usual actions of Creating Components, adding Traits, or narrating Events, the primary activity players will be engaged in while there is an open Complication is adding dice to the various Complication Dice Pools.

○ There are two ways to add dice to a Dice Pool:

1. Draw Upon a Trait.

2. Buy Dice Directly.

During their turn, any player can call for the Complication to be closed. If all other players agree (i.e. no player wishes to add any more dice) then the dice are rolled to resolve it. Following resolution, play continues with the player who closed the Complication.

ALIGNING COMPONENTS

All Components that are committed to a Complication (i.e. Traits have or will be Drawn Upon to provide dice to a Dice Pool) must be aligned with either the Source side or the Target side of the Complication.

93

When a Complication begins, the Originator will have designated one or more Components that they do not Control as Targets. All of those Components are automatically aligned with the Target side of the Complication and the players who currently Control those Components begin to build Target Dice Pools. If the Originator initiated the Complication on their own turn, then any Components they Control that are involved in trying to affect the Targets are aligned with the Source side of the Complication. If the Originator initiated the Complication on another player's turn by buying dice to serve as an obstacle, then those dice form the Source side of the Complication but there are no Source aligned Components yet. In either case, the Originator will be building a Source Dice Pool.

For example: During the final battle with the forces of Slytheran, Kevin McCrae is stationed in the Communications Bunker where he is helping to direct the defenses. It is Bob's turn.

Bob: Ok, I'm Taking Control of the Doom Cannon and General Von Stuben [2 Coins]. The General recognizes that the Meadow defenses are being centrally coordinated and orders the Doom Cannon to assault the Communications Bunker. [This costs 1 Coin for the General's observation and 1 Coin for the assault order. Since Bob doesn't Control the bunker this Originates a Complication. Bob declares that the Doom Cannon and General Von Stuben are the Sources of the Complication and that the Communication Bunker and Kevin McCrae are the Targets. Referring to the game record, the players note that Albert is in Control of the Communications Bunker, having Created it earlier in the scene, and Dave is currently in Control of Kevin. Therefore Bob, as the Originator, will be building a Source Pool while Albert and Dave are now declared on the Target side. The four identified Components are now committed and cannot be taken over for the rest of the Complication.]

Bob: I'm going to draw on a bunch of Traits from the Doom Cannon, let's see, *Doom Cannon, Hides, Armor,*

MORE THAN TWO SIDES IN A COMPLICATION

For simplicity, the rules refer to two sides, the Source side and the Target side. However, it is certainly possible to have multi-side Complications. This can occur any time the Originator identifies more than one Component Controlled by different players as Targets. Each player can declare their own Target Pool to be a separate side rather than aligned with the others. If it becomes necessary, players can declare which Target side they are aligned with in standard play order starting to the left of the Originator. Any other player who wants to involve one of their Components in the Complication can declare it for one of the existing sides, or start their own side.

When the dice are rolled, successes from each side are totaled separately. The single side with the most successes is the winning side, all others are losing sides. Losing sides narrate in order from most Bonus Coins to least. If a side has more than one Pool, each PoolPool within the side narrates from most Bonus Coins to least.

Accuracy, and *Assault Cannon x3.* I'm also going to take one for the *Control Chip* because that allows the attack to be precisely coordinated. [Bob counts out eight dice and adds them to his Pool]. Then, for the General, I'm going to take *General* because he's obviously giving orders in a battle, *Von Stuben* his proper name, and *Master Planner* for three more dice.

At this point, the rest of the Components in the scene are considered undeclared although they may have some natural alignments based on the nature of the Complication. Since the undeclared Components were not part of the initial narration that Originated the Complication, players who want to involve a Component they Control in the Complication will have to narrate an appropriate action on their turn to get them involved.

Once a Component is involved in the Complication, you declare which side it is on by Drawing Upon a Trait and adding a die to the appropriate side (or subtracting it from the opposing side). If you don't currently have a Dice Pool, you can involve it on either side. If you do currently have a Dice Pool, you can

95

MULTI-SIDE GIMMICKS:

Some common Gimmicks to consider when multi-side Complications are common in your games:

NO FALLOUT FROM ALLIES:

Normally, as the player narrating a Dice Pool, you can narrate freely any effect desired as long as it doesn't contradict any earlier narration from the Complication. This includes narrating a damaging or harmful effect to a Component on the same side as you. With this Gimmick that is no longer allowed. Instead, you can't narrate any effect to a Component Controlled by an allied player without that player's permission. In order to narrate such an effect freely, you'd have to be on different sides. Thus the advantage of being allied is combining Successes for a greater chance to win, but the disadvantage is a limit on narration.

PERMISSION TO ALLY:

This is common Gimmick if using the limiting Gimmick above. If it is your intention to narrate a damaging effect to a particular Component, you can refuse to allow the player Controlling that Component to ally with you. The player controlling the Pool with the most dice currently on that side (ties go the first player to join the side) gets to allow or disallow additional members.

only involve it on the side you're already a part of. Expect to be Challenged if your choice of side goes against any perceived natural alignment for that Component.

Any player can Take Over any currently undeclared Component, Introduce a Component not currently in the scene, or Create a new Component from scratch and begin to Draw Upon its Traits and declare alignment as above.

Continuing with the assault on the bunker:

Christine: Hmm, well I'm in control of the Meadow's Magnetic Accelerator Artillery Battery, and they're going to open fire on the advancing Doom Cannon, so I'm going to Draw Upon the *Artillery Battery*

Trait, as well as its *High Explosive Rounds,* to create a Target Pool with two Dice. [1 Coin for the action to open fire and thus get involved in the Complication. Being that the Component is part of the Meadow's defenses, its natural alignment is obvious and Christine doesn't try to go against that.]

Dave is already declared for the Target Side by way of Controlling Kevin, a Component specifically Targeted by the Originator. Dave spends his turn Drawing Upon Traits of Kevin's that would be appropriate for defending the bunker to build his own Target Dice Pool.

Ed is currently in Control of Turk Reigns, but instead of involving Turk in this Complication, Ed elects to Introduce a squad of Slytheran Shock Troopers for 1 Coin and narrate them advancing in support of the Doom Cannon for another Coin. He then begins Drawing Upon their applicable Traits and forming a Source Dice Pool on the same side as Bob.

Albert is already declared for the Target Side by way of Controlling the Communications Bunker, which was also targeted by Bob in the Complication. He also Controls a squad of Meadow Home Guard and, for 1 Coin, narrates them taking up position in the bunker. He then builds his Target Dice Pool using Traits Drawn Upon from the Bunker and the Home Guard.

ALIGNED COMPONENTS AND TAKE OVERS

Take Overs work essentially the same as described in Chapter 4, with the following restriction. During a Complication, Components that have been aligned with a side in the Complication are not available to be Taken Over. This rule is there to avoid the bizarre effects that could result from Components changing hands in the middle of a Complication.

○ Aligned Components can not be Taken Over.

○ Unaligned Components can be Taken Over as normal.

Aligned Components are defined as any Components that were identified as a Source or Target by the Originator when the Complication was Originated, and also any that have had

(97)

at least one Trait Drawn Upon from them during the current Complication.

If the Component is not yet aligned with a side, then Drawing Upon a Trait will align it. A Component cannot be aligned with a side different from that of its Controlling player. If its Controlling player is not yet aligned with a side, then aligning one of the player's Components will align the player. If the player is already aligned with the opposite side, then the Component's Traits cannot be Drawn Upon. It will either need to be aligned with the same side as its current Controller (if sensible) or Taken Over by another player who already is, or will become aligned with that side.

> Returning to the assault on the bunker; it is still Albert's turn. Albert recognizes that Turk Reigns is still Controlled by Ed, but now that Ed is aligned with the Slytheran in this Complication, Ed will not be able to Draw Upon any of Turk's Traits (unless Ed were to attempt to have Turk betray the Meadow to the Slytheran, which would be instantly Challenged by almost everyone at the table). Albert, who is already aligned with the Meadow side for this Complication, Takes Over Turk for 1 Coin and narrates "Kevin calls Turk on the communicator" [1 Coin] and "Turk responds by rushing to the bunker" [1 Coin]. Now that Turk's involved in the Complication, Albert can begin to Draw Upon his Traits as well.

> To prevent this, Ed, who was in Control of Turk during his turn, could have narrated "Turk is currently too far away to make it to the bunker in time to get involved in the battle" for 1 Coin. This would not have prevented Albert from Taking Over Turk, but it would have meant that when Albert attempted to have Turk rush to the bunker Ed could have Challenged with the weight of Fact behind him.

> **Bob:** Okay, also in the bunker is Lt. Chaunce [Lt. Chaunce is a minor existing character who is an aid to General Trudeau. Introducing him costs 1 Coin.] Unbeknownst to anyone, Chaunce has been having a Secret *Affair with Lady Alisandre*, the spy, and he *Has Been Seduced into Betraying the Meadow* [2

Coins for adding these two Traits to the Lieutenant.] Bob has now aligned Chaunce with the Source side of the Complication and can begin to Draw Upon his Traits to add to his own Dice Pool.

DRAW UPON TRAITS

○ Drawing Upon Traits is FREE if they can be narrated to apply to the current Complication.

○ This aligns the Component with one side or the other as appropriate to the narration.

○ The Component must be aligned with the same side as the Controlling player or the Trait cannot be Drawn Upon.

○ If the Trait is beneficial to the Component one die is added to the Controlling player's Dice Pool or subtracted from a Dice Pool aligned with the opposite side.

○ If the Trait is detrimental to the Component, one die is subtracted from the Controlling player's Dice Pool, or added to a Dice Pool aligned with the opposite side.

Drawing upon Traits is the primary (and most cost-effective) means of increasing the dice in a Dice Pool. Mechanically, this involves simply identifying an appropriate Trait that is present in the scene and which would apply in some fashion to the Complication at hand and narrating that application in the scene. Traits can be either beneficial or detrimental to their Component's interests.

If the Trait is beneficial to its Component, then when it is Drawn Upon a die is added to its Controlling player's Dice Pool (regardless of who Drew upon it). By definition, the Component and the Controlling player must be aligned with the same side in order for the Trait to be Drawn Upon. Alternatively, the drawing player can have the Trait subtract a die from any appropriate Dice Pool on the opposite side.

You can Draw Upon the Trait of any Component in the scene whether you Control them or not. However, the Trait must be used in a manner consistent with its nature and the Component that it is a part of. In many cases this consideration will dictate whether the Trait is beneficial or detrimental. A Trait such as *Great Strength* will, by its very nature, be beneficial to a char-

RULES GIMMICK: NO SUBTRACTING DICE

Contributed by Roy Penrod

The basic Complication rules allow for a Trait to be used to either add a die to a Pool or subtract a die from a Pool depending on the nature of the Trait and how the drawing player wants to interpret it.

This Gimmick restricts the option to adding dice only. Pools can never be reduced either by Drawing Traits or Buying Dice. While this restricts the options somewhat, it ensures there will never be empty Pool and encourages larger amounts of Bonus Coins to spend from the Complication.

On the down side, some play groups have found that after several sessions of play Components have acquired so many Traits that dice pools become very large and Complications are generating more Bonus Coins than the group desires. Having the ability to cancel dice rather than add them helps keep dice pools to a more manageable size.

Fortunately, Gimmicks can be turned off just as easily as they can be turned on.

---

acter involved in a wrestling match. A Trait such as *Coaching* will be beneficial to a coach helping his team win a game. A Trait such as *Sprained Ankle* will be detrimental to a character running a race. A Trait such as *Works Alone* could be narrated as being detrimental in a Complication where teamwork is required.

Often, whether a Trait is beneficial or detrimental will depend on the nature of the Complication. If the Trait could be interpreted either beneficially or detrimentally in the given circumstance, then the player who Draws Upon the Trait can decide how it gets used on that occasion. For instance, if the coach had been bribed to throw the game and so was declared on the opposite side of the Complication from his team, his *Coaching* Trait could go either way. If the team's player Draws Upon it, then they can explain how the previous good coaching the team has experienced has prepared them for the game and the Trait can be treated as detrimental to the coach. If the coach's or the opposing team's player Draws Upon it, then they can explain how the coach uses his ability to sabotage his team's efforts and the Trait can be treated as

(100)

beneficial to the coach. Similarly, the *Sprained Ankle* that would be an almost certain detriment in a foot race could be interpreted as beneficial (due the sympathy it engenders) to a Complication involving flirting. Or it might not be seen to apply at all to a Complication involving a chess game.

Whoever gets to it first (possibly a good time for an Interrupt) can decide how the Trait gets used.

> When the turn comes back around to Bob, he notices that Christine hadn't Drawn Upon the *Long Range* Trait for her artillery. Bob decides to Draw Upon that Trait himself but declares that because the Doom Cannons have penetrated deep into the Meadow lines that the range is too short for effective use. Therefore the *Long Range* Trait is actually a detriment to the artillery and Bob uses it to subtract a die from Christine's Dice Pool, leaving her with one.

> Later, the Slytheran win their assault on the communications bunker and, as part of narrating the victory, Bob describes the bunker (which was fully destroyed by paying Coins equal to its Importance) collapsing and trapping Kevin McCrae under the rubble. Kevin now has the Trait *Trapped Under Rubble*, which will serve as a Fact to Challenge any action that involves Kevin acting freely.

> Albert, who is in Control of Turk, now wants to narrate how Turk uses his *Strong* Trait to free Kevin from the rubble. However, he cannot simply remove the *Trapped under Rubble* Trait because he doesn't currently Control Kevin. So he Takes Over Kevin for 1 Coin in order to narrate the rescue [And remove the Trait for 1 Coin.]

> Ed, who is still in Control of a squad of Slytheran Troopers, however, intervenes and turns the rescue attempt into a Complication by buying dice representing the weight of the rubble and the difficulty in getting Kevin out. If he wins, he intends to narrate his Troopers coming upon the heroes in this awkward position and, if he has enough Coins, taking Kevin prisoner.

> Albert will thus begin a Target Dice Pool with Kevin and Turk aligned on the Target side while Ed has already

(101)

begun the Source Dice Pool with his purchased dice. Albert will Draw Upon both Kevin's and Turk's proper names and it is clear that, since both characters want to get Kevin out of the rubble, those Traits are beneficial to their Components and will be added to Albert's Dice Pool (even if Ed had Drawn Upon those Traits). Similarly, Turk's *Strong* Trait will go into Albert's Pool. It would be hard for Ed to narrate a reason explaining how being strong isn't an advantage for Turk in this situation. Similarly, if Turk also had obtained the Trait *Weakened From Injuries*, that die would obviously hinder his efforts and, if Drawn Upon, Albert would have a hard time narrating a reason for it to not subtract from his own Dice Pool or add to Ed's.

However, Kevin does have a *Pack Full of Gear* as a Trait. This one is more up in the air. Albert might be able to Draw Upon the Trait if he can justify there being something in the pack that would help. On the other hand, Ed might be able to Draw Upon that Trait by describing how the bulkiness of the pack (which as far as anyone knows, Kevin is still wearing) makes it more difficult to pull Kevin out because it keeps getting caught. Whoever thinks to Draw Upon the Trait first and can come up with a good justification that won't be Challenged will get the die for that Trait.

This is nothing more than the application of the standard rule that is true throughout Universalis: any action taken must be justified to the other players' satisfaction or risk being Challenged. To Draw Upon the Trait, the player must explain how that Trait applies to the situation described by the Complication. The nature of this description might then be used as justification to Draw Upon another Trait. The Challenge mechanic is always available to oppose uses of Traits that other players don't find justifiable. Also, Tenets may be used to provide guidelines as to the suitability or unsuitability of certain creative interpretations of Traits going forward.

A Trait can only be Drawn Upon once and provides only one die for any single Complication. If, however, the Component possesses the same Trait multiple times (i.e. if Turk had *Strong x2* as a

Trait) then each occurrence of the Trait can be Drawn Upon separately, providing additional dice. If a Component is involved in more than one Complication, its Traits can be used in all of them, but must be justified separately for each. Traits newly purchased during the Complication can be Drawn Upon immediately.

BUYING DICE

○ Buying dice costs 1 Coin to add or subtract one die to or from a Dice Pool.

Buying dice is the only other way of increasing (or decreasing) the number of dice in a Dice Pool. For 1 Coin, a die can be added to any Pool or an existing die removed from any Pool. Like everything else in the game, however, this purchase must be justified. Buying dice allows players to purchase modifiers for features, advantages, or disadvantages that are temporary to the scene or Event at hand and, unlike Traits, do not last beyond the Complication. If the player wants the feature to last it can be bought as a Trait. If the feature really isn't appropriate as a Trait (or is only appropriate as a Trait), other players may use the Challenge mechanic to see that it is accounted for properly.

Each time dice are bought, the player must provide a description of what the source of the modification is. This description may then provide justification for the activation of other Traits.

> For example: During one of several Complications that made up the final battle, Dave, on the Slytheran side, paid 2 Coins to remove two dice from Ed's Dice Pool, declaring "you are fighting at a disadvantage because the Slytheran forces have laid down smoke to cover their advance." Dave went a step further and declared he was treating the smoke like a weather effect and subtracting 2 Dice from each of the Target Pools for the same 2 Coins (see earlier example Gimmick on page 19). No one wanted to spend the Coins to challenge, so Dave's use of the Gimmick stood.

> Ed at that point was in Control of Marissa and Drew Upon Marissa's *IR Goggles* Trait to add a die back to his Pool. Ordinarily this Trait would have had no applicability to the scene since it was occurring during the day, but the nature of Dave's description provided the

(103)

RULES GIMMICK: INDIVIDUAL PLAYER POOLS

In a basic Complication, each player who has an involved Component will have a Dice Pool to roll during resolution. Players who don't have Components involved in the Complication can participate by adding dice to any of the existing Pools as they desire. However, it is the player who rolls the Pool who will benefit from any Bonus Coins from those dice.

This Gimmick allows every player who wants to participate to start their own Dice Pools (Source or Target Pools), even if they don't have an involved Component. They can buy dice for either side as normal, but instead of adding those dice to an existing Pool, they can keep them for their own Pool to roll and narrate themselves.

The advantage of this Gimmick is it gets all players involved in the narration and lets them win back the Coins they spent or even profit by it. The disadvantage is that it can encourage "frivolous" dice. In the standard rules, since you are paying for dice (or drawing on Traits) that will go into some other player's Pool for their benefit, you're only likely to do so if the actual outcome of the Complication is important to you.

Variant: In addition to the above, when Drawing Upon a Trait from a Component someone else Controls, you can add the die to your own Pool rather than the Controlling player's Pool as long as you're on the same side and the Trait could be said to benefit your Component as well.

justification, and so a Trait that wouldn't normally have applied now did.

RESOLVING THE COMPLICATION

Before the scene can end, the Complication must be resolved. Any player can call for the Complication to close on their turn. If none of the other players desire to do anything further in relation to the Complication, and all are satisfied with the Dice Pools as they stand (or at least are unwilling to spend more Coins to alter them further), resolution begins.

Each player who has a Dice Pool will roll that Pool. Each Dice Pool (and hence each player) will have been declared either as

---

**RULES GIMMICK:
USING d6s FOR COMPLICATIONS**

Contributed by Jonathan Nichol

The game uses d10s to resolve Complications. d10s are dice that have ten sides and are available in any local hobby or game shop where Role Playing Games are sold. However, for groups that don't have access to d10s (or enough of them) this Gimmick allows the game to be played with ordinary six sided cubes found in many typical board or casino games.

Build the Dice Pools with d6s exactly as you would for d10s. When the dice are rolled read any odd result (1, 3, or 5) as a Success. This has the same 50% possibility of getting a Success and also will provide the same average number of Bonus Coins to the winning side.

---

part of the Source side or as part of the Target side.

All of the Pools on the same side are counted together for purposes of determining which side wins the Complication. Each player's individual Pools are counted separately for purposes of spending the Coins generated (with each rolling player spending the results of their own Pool).

These standard Complication rules are robust enough to handle (in abstract form) nearly any Complication that could arise. For those who want more customized Complications, advanced Complication rules and more can be found on the Universalis website (http://ramshead.indie-rpgs.com). Players should also feel free to make use of Rules Gimmicks to address unique situations they'd like to handle differently.

○ The dice are d10s (10-sided) with '0' being read as '10.'

○ Each die that rolls a 1-5 (50% possibility) is a Success and is kept; any dice that roll 6-10 are set aside.

○ The side with the most Successes is the winner, the other side is the loser.

The side with the most Successes "wins" the Complication and will have the advantage in describing the results. A number of Bonus Coins are generated by the roll for each side and will be spent to narrate the results using standard game rules.

IF SUCCESSES ARE TIED

If both sides have the same number of Successes, add up the sum of the numbers on the Successful dice in each Pool. The side with the highest total has the Edge. Add one free die to that side and re-roll both sides. Continue re-rolling (giving out an additional Edge die each time) until the tie is broken. If the sum of the Successes is also tied, give an Edge die to each side and re-roll.

When there are multiple Pools on a side, give the Edge die to the Pool that contributed the most number of Successes to its side's cause. If this is tied, give the Edge die to the player sitting closest to the Originator clockwise around the table.

In resolving the Complication, players should treat ties as escalating drama and suspense and work this into the narrative accordingly.

> During the final battle, there is a Complication involving a firefight between teams of Meadow Soldiers and Slytheran Shock Troopers. Both sides are evenly matched, and both sides have six dice in their Pool.
>
> The dice are rolled and the results are: Source (Slytheran) 1, 3, 5, 6, 6, and 9 and Targets (Meadow) 2, 2, 3, 7, 8, and 9. Both sides have three Successes so there is a tie. The Slytheran have a sum of 1+3+5 = 9, however, while the Meadow has 2+2+3 = 7. The Slytheran have the advantage and so gain an Edge Die.
>
> Both sides re-roll, the Slytheran now with 7 dice. The results are 2, 3, 4, 6, 7, 7, and 10 for the Slytheran and 4, 5, 5, 8, 8, 9 for the Meadow. Again there is a tie at 3 Successes each. This time the Meadow has the Edge with 4+5+5 = 14 vs. 2+3+4 = 9 for the Slytheran.
>
> Both sides re-roll and now each have 7 dice their Pools. This time the results are: Slytheran: 1, 4, 5, 7, 7, 9 and 10 and Meadow: 2, 3, 4, 4, 8, 8, and 9. The Meadow has four successes to the Slytheran's three and thus wins the Complication.
>
> The Meadow forces won with four Successes: 2, 3, 4, and 4. As the winning side, they get 13 Bonus Coins to spend (the sum of the successful dice) on narrating the

result of the Complication. The Slytheran rolled seven dice. As the losing side, they get 7 Bonus Coins to spend (one for each die rolled) on narrating the result of the Complication.

As the winner, the Meadow has the advantage of going first and ensuring that they narrate the outcome of the Complication as they please. But the Slytheran will then get to spend their Coins on mitigating their losses or on making the Meadow pay for its victory.

It's important as the winning side that you spend those Bonus Coins on making what you want to happen, happen; and on declaring Facts to ensure that something you don't want to happen, doesn't. Anything that the winning side leaves up in the air is fair game for the losing side to narrate about.

COINS GENERATED

○ Each losing Pool generates 1 Bonus Coin per die rolled regardless of Success.

○ Each winning Pool generates a number of Bonus Coins equal to the total sum of all Successful dice in the Pool.

The winners will typically earn more (averaging 1.5 Coins per die) than the 1 Coin per die of the loser's Pool, which is part of the economic advantage of trying to win Complications. The winners will also get to narrate first. However, it's possible for the winners to earn less, meaning it is possible to win the Complication but wind up with fewer Coins, which is the risk of Complications.

USING THE COINS

○ The winners will spend their Coins first, in order from the player who earned the most Bonus Coins to the least. Ties are broken in favor of the player sitting closest to the Complication Originator in clockwise order.

○ On their turn, winning players may spend their Coins to narrate the resolution of the Complication. They may also spend their Coins to eliminate Coins from the losing pool of their choice on a one-for-one basis.

○ The losers will then spend their Coins (any not elimi-

RULES GIMMICK: NO NEGATING BONUS COINS

One of the uses for Bonus Coins won by the winning side in a Complication is to negate, one for one, Bonus Coins won by the losing side. This rule allows the winning side to reduce or even eliminate the chance of the losers narrating negative fallout on winning Components by giving up some of their own ability to make things happen. It represents taking a sort of defensive or cautious stance where not much is accomplished but not much is risked.

This Gimmick eliminates that option. It ensures that the losing side will always get some say in the results of the Complication and makes sure that every Complication carries risk even to the winning side.

nated by the winners) in order starting with the losing player with the most Bonus Coins down to the least. Ties are broken in favor of the player sitting closest to the Complication Originator in clockwise order.

○ Coins not spent can be added to the player's Wealth.

It is important to keep in mind that the dice rolled do not represent the success or failure of the involved Components directly. They are not a "skill check" or a "see if you can do that" check. Rather they are a roll off between the players to determine which player gets to decide what happens. The outcome is weighted in favor of the side which has the most relevant Traits to Draw Upon and in favor of the players who invested the most Coins and effort to accumulate the larger Dice Pools.

The narration of what happens must be consistent with the Traits used and biased in favor of the Components on the winning side, but does not have to directly result in the winning Components achieving all of their goals.

For instance, in a Complication involving a group of policemen attempting to apprehend some criminals, the player Controlling the police wins the roll. The police won and the goal of the police was clearly to arrest all of the criminals. But that doesn't mean that this is the goal of the player. The player is engaged in crafting a story and should be more concerned with making the story interesting for the real people around the table than in worrying about what the fictitious policemen want. In this case, even though the player Controlling the police won

RULES FOR USING COINS FROM COMPLICATIONS

1) Each player with a Pool on the winning side narrates the Bonus Coins generated by their Pool in order from the Pool with the most Bonus Coins to the least (ties being broken clockwise from the Originator).

2) A winning player may sacrifice any number of his own Bonus Coins to negate a like number of Bonus Coins from any combination of losing Pools desired.

3) Each player with a Pool on the losing side then narrates the Bonus Coins generated by their Pool in order from the Pool with the most Bonus Coins to the least (ties being broken clockwise from the Originator).

4) The Coins should be spent on items tied directly or indirectly to the Complication itself, not on narrating completely unrelated events or affecting completely unrelated Components.

5) The overall outcome should be narrated with a bias favoring the Components of the side that won or to the detriment of the Components of the side that lost.

6) The events and activities narrated should tie into or reference (at least tangentially) the Traits that were Drawn Upon and the justification given for purchased dice.

7) A player cannot be Interrupted while spending the Bonus Coins from a Complication and cannot add additional Coins from his own Wealth while resolving it.

the Complication he uses his Bonus Dice to narrate the criminals escaping but not before giving one of them a *Wound That Requires Medical Attention* and declaring that "the police have discovered the leader's identity after his mask slipped off during the fight." Both of these items will provide the opportunity for more dramatic moments in the future.

The Bonus Coins can be used in any and all ways already described in these rules. This includes: Creating a Component, adding Traits to a Component, removing or restoring Traits to a Component, overcoming Importance, narrating Events, Introducing additional Components into the scene, changing the location or even the time of the scene, and even proposing new game Tenets.

The only restriction is that the use of the Coins must be appropriate to the Complication at hand and bear some relation to the Traits that were Drawn Upon and the justifications used to purchase dice. The generated Coins can also be kept by the player and added to his own Wealth. In fact, Originating Complications is one way for a player short of Coins to earn a few additional ones.

THE BIG COMPLICATION EXAMPLE:

Following their escape from the forest fire, the heroes were in a quandary. They needed to get back across the river and back to Meadow in time to warn the town of the impending attack. Yet confronting them were troops dispatched by the Slytheran Queen with orders to stop them.

Its Albert's turn and he has just narrated how the team has moved downstream away from the fire and will be crossing the river on a hastily built pontoon boat with a tent cloth for a sail. He Created the boat as a Component with the Traits of *Pontoon Boat*, *Sturdy*, *Tent Cloth Sail*, *Bark Chip Paddles*, and *Big Enough for 3 Plus Gear*. He has narrated the boat being in the water and crossing the stream when he is Interrupted by Bob.

Bob: As the team tries to cross the river they are met by a hail of fire from the opposite bank. I'm Introducing two Squads of Slytheran Shock Troopers to oppose the crossing, which will make a Complication out of it. [He pays 4 Coins for each squad using both the Sub Component and Group Trait rules from Chapter 5.]

Drawing Upon the Traits from the Shock Trooper Master Component [See the example on page 72.], the squads each have *Shock Troopers*, *Fierce Fighters*, *Single Mindedly Aggressive*, and *High-Power Assault Rifle*. I think those all apply to the situation of trying to gun down the heroes on their little raft before they can cross. That's a total of four dice

(110)

per squad, or eight dice total for my Source Pool.

Plus I'm going to spend 2 Coins to buy two more dice representing the advantage of them ambushing you. Also, numbers are certainly an advantage here, and each squad has *Shock Squad x3* which I'll Draw Upon for six more dice. That brings me to 16. [Bob decides that the Troopers' *Acute Viper-like Sensing Pits* don't help because the targets are easily visible. Nor do their *Venomous Fangs* help since they aren't fighting at close quarters. The Troopers are *Blindingly Loyal* but so far neither their loyalty nor their morale has been called into question. They are equipped with *Body Armor* but the Targets haven't declared they're shooting back, so that doesn't apply yet either.]

Christine, Dave & Ed all take their turn in that order around the table, and all pass in order to wait and see how Albert decides to address this threat. [Having framed and narrated the entire scene, Albert is in Control of all of the characters at this point. Since Bob names the heroes and their raft as Targets for the Complication, they are now aligned with the Target side and can not be Taken Over by any other player as long as this Complication remains open. Traits from all four Components will be added to Albert's Target Pool.]

Albert: Wow, that's a hefty Complication, Bob. One might think you really want the Slytheran to win. Ok, let's start with the obvious choices. First, all three of the Targeted characters are named and so provide a die each. They each have Roles, but only Turk's Special Forces Trait seems applicable to the situation at hand, so that's a fourth die.

I guess we need to decide how they're going to respond to this danger. Going toe to toe in a firefight seems pretty futile (especially since Turk no longer has his weapon), so instead I think the team will decide to try and escape downstream, outrunning the troops on the shore and finding a safer place to land. So that gives us Turk's *Small Boat Handling* Trait, and

the Traits *Sturdy* and *Tent Cloth Sail* from the boat to add 3 more dice. [Turk's Trait had been added earlier during the snapping turtle scene when the players needed a way to get across the pond. Bob considers Challenging the use of the sail, since he doubts a jury-rigged piece of canvas will do much to speed up a raft heading downstream already, but decides it isn't worth making an issue out of it. Albert's choice of how the heroes will respond to the threat helped determine which Traits are applicable and which are not. Likewise, noticing that the party currently has many more Traits that would help them run than would help them fight, informs Albert of the best way to respond if he wants to win the Complication. Albert doesn't have to spend Coins on this decision because the act of running hasn't actually happened and can't until the Complication is resolved.]

Bob: I think the Complication is good where it is. [He decides to hold off adding any more dice to his Pool.]

Christine: Well, Marissa has *Fiercely Determined*. That sounds useable so a die for that. [Christine doesn't Control Marissa, so she doesn't get to start a Dice Pool of her own (they aren't playing with the Individual Player Pools Gimmick). This die gets added to Albert's Target Pool since he's in Control of Marissa currently (it could have also been subtracted from Ben's Complication Pool).] What about her *Command Ability*? Could she add a die for that, or not? [Here Christina is soliciting opinions about the suitability of a particular Trait.]

Bob: I don't think so, they're on a boat, and Marissa has no particular boating skill. It's more Turk's bailiwick at the moment. [The other players concur with this, and so no die is added.]

Dave: I pass.

Ed: What about Fritz? Kevin sends Fritz aloft to scout the far bank and signal when he's found a safe place to land. I'd say that counts for four dice: *Highly*

Trained, Embedded Control Chip, the proper name *Fritz* which we've been counting, and *Flies* from the Master Component of *Skylars.*

Bob: Man you're really milking that pet thing aren't you. You should have named him Lassie.

Ed: We've used him to scout stuff out before.

Bob: I'll tell you what, I give you two dice for it, but not four. Take one for being *Highly Trained* and one for the name. I still say its silly to give a pet that name bonus, but I already lost that Challenge. But the *Embedded Control Chip* and the *Flying* thing are what makes using Fritz even possible. Those Traits are your justification for getting any dice at all so I don't think its right to count them too. [Bob is Challenging Ed's use of Fritz here and is currently Negotiating with him on the appropriate number of dice. The other players think Bob's reasoning here is pretty flimsy, because that logic could apply to a lot of different situations and they've never treated Traits that way before, but when Christine points out that regardless of the reasoning, she doesn't like the idea of the pet overshadowing the heroes, they decide not to fight him on it. Only two dice are added to Albert's Target Pool. Because Fritz is owned by Kevin, and Albert currently Controls Kevin, Albert also automatically Controls Fritz. If Fritz wasn't owned by Kevin, since he hasn't been specifically targeted by the Complication yet, Ed could pay 1 Coin to Take Control of Fritz and start his own Target Pool. But in this case these dice go to Albert's Pool as well.]

Albert: Well, that gives me ten dice total. Let's go ahead and roll and see what happens.

Albert rolls the ten dice in his Target Pool. They come up 1, 1, 3, 5, 7, 9, 9, 10, 10, and 10.

Bob rolls 16 dice. They come up 1, 2, 2, 3, 4, 4, 5, 5, 5, 7, 7, 8, 8, 8, 9, and 10.

The Source Side wins with nine Successes to the Target's four.

That gives the Source Side 1+2+2+3+4+4+5+5+5 = 31 Bonus Coins, and the Target gets 10 [One per die rolled.]

Bob: Ok, this is what happens.

Coin 1: Blazing fire from the shore strikes the small craft repeatedly. Cross off the boat's *Sturdy* Trait. [1 Coin to Remove a Trait.]

Coin 2: Turk attempts to get the boat turned downstream. [Event for 1 Coin.]

Coin 3: But fire rips through the sail and cuts into the mast. Cross off the boat's *Tent Cloth Sail* Trait. [1 Coin to Remove a Trait.]

Coins 4 and 5: Meanwhile Slytheran Troopers spot the Skylar and recognize its providing aerial recon. [By this group's established standards, spotting the Skylar and recognizing the threat it poses are two separate Events for 1 Coin apiece.]

Coins 6 to 11: They open fire on it. Fritz dodges and weaves but it is ultimately futile. Two blasts hit the lizard in rapid succession and Fritz is incinerated. Kevin gets a "signal not found" error from his control chip [Fritz has a total Importance of 6, so 6 Coins is enough to Eliminate him from play and give Bob up to 6 Facts to describe the demise.]

Coins 12 and 13: The boat has started to make decent progress downstream despite the Troopers' running to keep up and it is starting to outdistance them. [The boat's progress and outdistancing the Troopers are two Events for 1 Coin each. There is some discussion as to whether the Troopers' running should be a third Event. Dave suggests that the running could be making them tired. But Bob decides its just Color and suggests Albert can pay for the Troopers being tired himself if he wants. Since no one Challenges, 2 Coins it is.

Coins 14 to 16: But the damage done to the boat is making it difficult to control, and when a last few parting shots strike home, the boat breaks apart and capsizes. [The pontoon boat initially had an Importance of 5, but 2 of its Traits have been Removed, reducing its Importance to 3. For 3 Coins Bob Eliminates the boat from play again getting up to 3 Facts to describe its destruction.]

Coins 17 to 22: The team is dumped into the water, and, with no boat, is carried much farther downstream than they'd intended. They are now farther away from the Meadow than they were when they started the crossing. [Bob initially pays for this as two Events for 1 Coin each and 1 Coin for the Fact that the team is now farther from the Meadow. Albert Challenges this believing Bob should pay for each of these items separately for each of the three team members. Ed, Dave, and Christine each voice their opinion. In the end it is decided through Negotiation that being dumped into the water should actually be free Color since it has already been established that the team was in the boat and the boat sank. Being swept down stream, and being farther away from the Meadow will apply separately to each team member since they are separate Components. Thus, instead of 3 Coins, Bob will pay 6.]

Coin 23 to 27: Let's see that leaves me with just 9 Bonus Coins to go. I'll use 5 of them to negate 5 of your Coins, Albert; leaving you with 5. [Negating the losing side's Coins one for one is one of the uses for the winner's Bonus Coins.]

Coin 28 to 31: And I'll keep the remaining 4 Coins for myself offsetting some of my cost for setting up this Complication. [Adding Coins to Wealth is another use for Bonus Coins.] Oh wait, I'll use one of those Coins to give the *Soaking Wet* Trait to everyone again for being dunked in the river [See the example Gimmick on page 19].

Dave: Oh my god, you killed Fritz, you bastard!

Ed: Poor Fritz, he was a good lizard.

Albert: Ok, with 5 Coins I can't do much, which was obviously Bob's intention. So, first things first.

> **Coins 1-3:** All three team members manage to make it safely to the desired shore, so they're now on the right side of the river. [3 Coins for each character crossing the river. The safely part comes as a result of Bob not seeing fit to saddle the characters with any injury so Albert isn't about to either.]

> **Coin 4:** Turk recognizes where they are, so they aren't lost. [1 Coin to establish that as Fact so they can at least avoid that difficulty going forward.]

> **Coin 5:** And finally, none of their gear appeared to be lost or damaged in the dunking [One could argue that this should require a separate Coin for each character whose gear made it safely through, but no one Challenges, so Albert gets it for a single Coin.]

Albert ends the scene, and after a round of bidding, Dave wins the right to frame the next one. He decides to continue where the previous one left off and so begins his scene with the wet and bedraggled heroes having just crawled up on the river bank. Christine then Interrupts and Takes Over Marissa and starts narrating her leading them away from the river. Bob then Interrupts Christine and starts another Complication.

Bob: I'm Creating *Buzzers*. They are the somewhat *Larger*, More *Aggressive*, *Carnivorous*, *Cousins of Skylars*. They also *Fly*, but they eat meat instead of fruit. They have a *Paralytic Venom*, that they can *Spray at Their Target*, which allows them to leech on and *Suck Their Prey Dry* in safety. They also have *Embedded Control Chips* and are used as *Aerial Weapons* by the Slytheran [Bob pays 11 Coins for the above Traits, plus a 12th to make buzzers a Master Component. Ed wonders if this Component doesn't derive from Bob wanting to introduce Fritz's evil twin.]

I'm saying there is a bunch of them, so I'm Creating a Sub

art © 2002, david hedgecock

Jerek and his War Sparrow "Fright" drive off the attacking Buzzers.

Component Buzzer with a Numbers x3 Trait for 4 Coins.

They've been following the team's progress down the river, and seeing them make it to shore alive, they descend to finish the job. [2 Coins for the following and the descent as Events. Clearly "finish the job" indicates an intent to do harm to the heroes so this initiates another Complication. Up until now, the creation of the buzzers was just an exercise in Component Creation.]

Dave: Dang, that's 18 Coins you sunk into this Complication.

Christine: Yeah, and he's Created another weapon for the Slytheran army to attack the Meadow with. Now they have an air force too.

Bob: Ok, *Large, Aggressive, Carnivorous, Fly, Paralytic Venom, Spray at Their Target, Suck Their Prey Dry, Control Chips,* and *Aerial Weapons.* That's nine dice plus three from the Group Trait, giving me 12 dice for my Source Pool.

Christine: Are we going to fight them?

Dave: Yeah, I guess we have no choice this time.

Christine: Ok, well then, I'm then going to Draw Upon Marissa's *Command Ability*, and her *Laser Pistol*. I'm not going to Draw Upon her *Trained Killer x2* because I don't think that covers flying lizards. But I do think *Hard Cold Demeanor* can work. I see this as being one of those grim moments where the camera focuses on her standing there all calm, cool, and collected barking orders and taking charge. I'll also take a die for her Name. [That gives Christine a Target Pool of 4 dice. Her description of Marissa's attitude was her explanation for why the *Demeanor* Trait applies and as such is just Color.]

Bob: That works for me,

Dave: What about her *Determination*?

Christine: Well, you can Draw Upon that if you want, but it seems to me that since there is no clear objective like crossing the river to this scene that I don't think it applies. I'm done for now. [There are no hard and fast rules for when a Trait applies and when it doesn't. But in this game, the group has established through precedent that Marissa's *Determination* Trait is only used when Marissa's has a specific goal to focus on, so by that convention, Christine elects not to use it here.]

Dave: Hmmm, we'll see. So, I'll Draw Upon Turk's and Kevin's Name Traits for two dice, plus Turk's *Special Forces* Training. Then I'll pass. Now what? [Dave starts his own Target Pool with 3 dice.]

Ed: Beats me. I pass too.

Albert: Time to call in the big guns. I'm paying 1 Coin to Introduce Jerek into the scene. That also brings in the sparrow he rides automatically as a possession. He's been shadowing us ever since he watched the snakes start that fire, and now he's seen our plight and decided to come in guns blazing. [Albert pays the 1

Coin for the Introduction, plus 2 more for the Events that Jerek has been following and that he leaps into the fray. This now aligns Jerek with the Target side.]

Let's see. He's got *Ace Flyer x3,* and his sparrow is *Cybernetically Enhanced* and has *Mounted Laser Cannons Across the Neck x2.* That's six dice total. Plus I'm going to take one for Jarek's Name. I'm not going to take one for Fright's name because we haven't really treated Fright like a character the way we did for poor old Fritz, but I am going to buy two dice for his surprise attack out of the sun. [By Introducing and aligning a new Component to the Complication, Albert can start a Target Pool of his own with 9 dice in it.]

Bob: Sweet, I wondered if that rogue was ever going to show up. I figured he might if I threw a flying enemy at the heroes.

Christine: Hooray for Jerek! I wonder if this will change Marissa's feelings for him. I don't have anything more to do.

Dave: Don't know, but I think that his showing up is enough of a justification to trigger Marissa's *Fiercely Determined* Trait. She's not going to want to admit she needed Jarek to rescue her. So I'm going to Draw Upon that. By my count that should give the team 17 total dice. [Since Marissa is Controlled by Christine, the extra die Dave Draws Upon goes to her Pool, making it five. Three in Dave's Pool, and nine in Albert's does indeed give the Target side 17 total dice.]

Ed: I say we roll, Bob you want to add anything else?

Bob: Let's roll.

Christine rolls her 5 dice and they come up: 1, 3, 5, 7, and 10 for three Successes.

Dave rolls his 3 dice and they come up: 2, 4, and 8 for two Successes.

119

Albert rolls his 9 dice and they come up: 2, 3, 4, 4, 5, 5, 6, 8, and 9 for six Successes.

Bob rolls his 12 dice for the Complication which come up: 1, 3, 5, 5, 6, 6, 6, 8, 8, 8, 9, and 10 for four Successes.

The Target side wins with 11 total Success to four. Albert receives 23 Bonus Coins and will narrate first for the winning side. Christine receives 9 Bonus Coins and will narrate second for the winning side. Dave receives 6 Bonus Coins and will narrate third for the winning side. Bob receives 12 Bonus Coins (one per die rolled) and will narrate for the losing side.

We'll end the example here in the interest of brevity. Suffice it to say that after a brilliant dog fight and a saving shot from Marissa's pistol, all of the buzzers were shot down. Jerek then offered to take the heroes back to Meadow the short way if they help him get his commission reinstated in the air wing (you'll recall he'd been exiled for some, as yet still unspecified, crime). Ultimately the heroes agreed, and with Marissa riding behind him in the saddle, and Turk and Kevin dangling painfully from Flight's claws (although less painfully than having been left to the Slytheran Troopers who were still closing in), the team returns to Meadow in time to put the defenses on full alert.

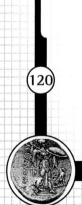

CONCLUSION

Now you have everything you need to create your own worlds and characters with Universalis. You're ready to see what kind of story comes out of the collective imagination of you and your friends. You'll find that the more you play Universalis, the more the system becomes second nature and fades into the background, and the more you will begin to use it in new and unexpected ways. This is a natural part of the process of acclimating to these rules. In other words, the more you play, the more Universalis molds itself to become the game you want it to be. This effect should not be overlooked. Universalis, over time, actually becomes the game it needs to be to fit your style of play. Try the system out "as is" for a bit, but don't be afraid to add in a Gimmick whenever you feel the need. Make the game play how you want it to play for you and your group. Get creative with its use, and you'll like the results.

> What will happen to the heroes in our example? Will they be able to lead the Meadow forces to victory? Will the Slytheran conquer the Meadow and lead to a sequel featuring Lady Alisandre as the Queen's governor tormenting poor Turk? How will their story end? We don't know; it hasn't been played out. That's a very fun part of Universalis, nobody ever really knows where the story is going until it gets there. You could play out the end of the Meadow gang if you wanted to. Better yet, make up your own world, heroes, and story. You'll find that it's more rewarding than you might have imagined.

Be sure to check out the Universalis Website at: http://www.ramshead.indie-rpgs.com where you'll find:

○ Add-ons...pre-designed Rules Gimmicks that can be incorporated directly into your game

○ Links to the Universalis Forum on The Forge where you can have your game questions answered

○ Essays and game guides on how to get the most out of your Universalis sessions

We also want to see transcripts of your games, great scenes you've run, and characters, locations, and props you've created. If we like them, we'll put them up on the page where everyone can use them as a source of inspiration for their own games.

Happy Gaming,
— Ralph & Mike

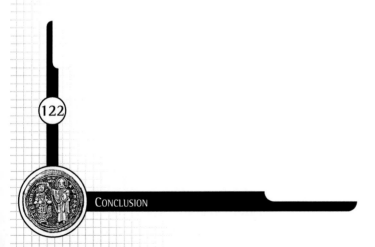

CONCLUSION

GLOSSARY
& INDEX

Add-on: A Rules Gimmick that has been standardized and recorded so that it can be easily included in future games. (121)

Bank: A central reserve of Coins where all spent Coins are returned and new Coins are drawn from. (11)

Bid for Turn: Players bid secretly for the right to frame the next scene. The winner is the Framing Player and can spend the Coins bid during the scene. The losers return their bid to their Wealth. Ties are broken by the first player to the left of the last Framing Player. (22)

Bidding in Challenges: If Negotiations fail to resolve a Challenge, players Bid. The Challenging player must bid first (openly) followed in order by the other players, with the Challenged player bidding last. Each player can bid one or more Coins either in favor of the Challenger or the Challenged (or a new option). The side with the most Coins when no one wishes to bid further wins. If a Fact is being contradicted, Coins spent on defending the Fact count double for the Challenge. (37)

Bonus Coins: Coins won in a Complication and used to narrate the outcome. Each player on the winning side gets a number of Bonus Coins equal to the sum of the numbers on their Success dice. Each player on the losing side gets a number of Bonus Coins equal to the number of dice they rolled. Narrations go in order from most Bonus Coins received to fewest, with all winners narrating before any of the losing side. Ties are broken in clockwise order from the Originator. (107)

Buying Dice: 1 Coin allows one die to be added to or subtracted from any Dice Pool. The rationale for this must be fully justified by the player making the purchase. (103)

Challenge: A means for players to regulate the actions of other players in the game. Any action or behavior can be Challenged. If possible, the issue is resolved through Negotiation. If not, it is resolved by Bidding Coins. (34)

Characters: A type of Component describing a person or group of people (where person is defined very loosely). Characters are the most important Component, and the story is told through them. Players can Control any character in the story; there are no specific player characters. (57)

Coins: Coins regulate story power in the game. Players spend them to add Traits to Components, Tenets to the game, and narrate Events in scenes. Additional Coins can be earned from Complications and automatic Refreshment after every scene. (12)

Color: Color is anything a player says while narrating that they do not pay a Coin for. Color is not considered to be Fact, and can never be written down as a Trait. Other players are not obligated to abide by anything said that is just Color. But Color allows a player to add interesting and entertaining but mechanically superfluous details without spending unnecessary amounts of Coin. (10, 47)

Complication: Once a player Originates a Complication, players Controlling an involved Component can build Dice Pools by Buying Dice or Drawing Upon Traits. When all players are finished, Complications are resolved by rolling the Pools and counting Successes. The side with the most Successes wins and both sides receive Bonus Coins to narrate the outcome. (50, 88)

Component: All people, places, and things, and even intangibles can be defined as Components. All Components are collections of Traits that describe it. The more Traits, the more Important the Component is to the story. If it is a noun it can be defined as a Component. (9, 57)

Control: The player who Introduces a Component into a scene Controls that Component until it is Taken Over by another player. Only the Controlling player can add, Remove, or Restore Traits to a Component or involve a Component in an Event without causing a Complication. (49)

Create Component: Players Create all Components in the game by purchasing one or more Traits for it costing 1 Coin each. The first Trait must be the Component's Role. (57)

Damage Trait: A specific kind of Trait that is added to a Component to represent injury or damage of some kind. During the game, Events involving the Component should be narrated to take the Damage Trait into account. During Complications, the Damage Trait can be Drawn Upon to provide dice that hinder the Component if applicable. Damage Traits do increase Importance while present and can be healed or repaired by paying to Remove them (which reduces Importance). (82)

Dialog: When a Character Controlled by one player wishes to have a conversation with a Character Controlled by another, the two (or more) players can enter into Dialog with the initiating player paying 1 Coin. During Dialog, the players speak in the voices of their Characters and pay for any statements their Characters make that they wish to have treated as Fact. (52)

Dice Pool: In a Complication, every player who Controls a Component will have a Dice Pool of d10s declared in favor of either the Source side or the Target side. Dice are added to the Pools on a player's turn either buy Buying them or Drawing Upon Traits. (92)

Drawing Upon Traits: Any Component in a scene can have its Traits Drawn Upon during a Complication. If a particular Trait applies to the Complication at hand, it can add or subtract one die to the relevant Dice Pool. Each Trait can provide only one die per Complication but can be used in multiple Complications in any one scene. (59, 99)

Edge Dice: If the number of Successes rolled in a Complication are tied, sum the values of each of the Success dice on each side. The side with the highest total gets a free Edge Die added to whichever Pool on that side contributed the most Successes (ties broken clockwise from the Originator). The Pools of both sides are then re-rolled. Continue re-rolling and adding Edge Dice until the tie is broken. If the sum of the Success dice are also tied, add an Edge Die to each side and re-roll. (106)

Eliminated: Components can be Eliminated from the game by paying Coins equal to their Importance. Each Coin paid also entitles the player to a Fact regarding the Component's fate. Eliminated Components cannot be Introduced into any scene occurring chronologically after the time of its Elimination. They can be returned to play (with suitable justification) by paying additional Coins equal to their Importance. (79)

Event: Events cost 1 Coin and deliver the action of the story. Each Event consists of a single effect, a single Component receiving the effect,

(125)

and/or a single Component performing the effect. If Components are nouns and Traits are adjectives, then Events are verbs. (44)

Exit Component: Exiting a Component is the opposite of Introducing a Component. With a suitable justification, a Component currently present in a scene can be removed from the scene for 1 Coin. (26, 27)

Facts: Facts cost 1 Coin and give added leverage in Challenges. A Trait is a Fact assigned to a Component. A Tenet is a Fact assigned to the game itself. An Event is a Fact assigned to a scene. (8, 10, 39)

Fines: Fines are a way of indicating dissatisfaction with the play of another player. Any player can at any time call for a Fine against another player. All players vote simultaneously "thumbs-up" to levy the Fine or "thumbs-down" if no Fine is necessary. The losing party must pay a number of Coins equal to the total thumbs against them to the Bank. (42)

Framing Player: The winner of the Bid for Turn is the Framing Player. They can use the Coins they bid (and additional ones from Wealth) to Frame the Scene. They cannot be Interrupted while doing this. The first Event they narrate ends framing and begins regular play. Only the Framing Player can declare a scene ended. (24)

Framing a Scene: The Framing Player Frames a Scene by Establishing Location, Setting the Time, and Introducing Components. They cannot be Interrupted while doing so. The Framing ends when the Framing Player narrates the first Event. (25, 26)

Group Trait: Any Component can be turned into a group of like Components simply by adding a Group Trait. The number of times the Group Trait is added indicates the relative numbers of the group (not necessarily at a 1:1 ratio). The additional numbers are not treated separately in the game (it is still a single Component) but the Trait can be Drawn Upon in any Complication where additional numbers would be useful. (63)

Importance: All Components have an Importance, which is simply equal to one for every non-Removed Trait the Component has, plus the Importance of any Possessions it owns. A Component can only be Eliminated from the game if a number of Coins equal to this Importance is spent to do so (and can be justified).

Likewise, an Eliminated Component can be brought back into the game if a number of Coins equal to its Importance is spent to do so (and can be justified). (78)

Interrupt: For 1 Coin, any player can Interrupt the turn of another player (except during Framing or when spending Bonus Coins while resolving a Complication) and begin taking his own turn. The Interrupted player can finish his immediate thought before handing over the turn. (30)

Introduce Component: Any existing Component can be Introduced into a scene by paying 1 Coin. Any new Component can be automatically Introduced into a scene by the same Coin that Created it. Only Components that have been Introduced can have Traits Drawn Upon for Complications. (26)

Locations: A type of Component describing a place. Locations are one of the first things that must be Established in any scene for 1 Coin. (25)

Losing Side: The side rolling fewer Successes in a Complication. Each player on the Losing Side gets 1 Bonus Coin for every die they rolled to narrate the outcome of the Complication, after the Winning Side's narration is completed. (105)

Master Component: A Component can be marked as a Master Component for 1 Coin. A Component so marked can never be given a Proper Name and serves as a template for every related Sub Component tied to it. The Traits bought for the Master Component should be suitable for a generic representative of that class or category of Components. A Master Component cannot be eliminated unless all of its Sub Components have been eliminated. (70)

Mini Scene: Instead of waiting for the current scene to end and then winning the next Bid for Turn, a player, on their turn, can cut to a scene elsewhere to depict events going on in another time or place. The Mini Scene automatically ends at the end of the player's turn (voluntarily or by Interruption). There is no additional cost for the Mini Scene, but Establishing a Location, Setting a Time, and Introducing Components all cost as they do for framing a normal scene. (32)

Negotiation: Before any Challenge goes to Bidding, players can discuss alternative solutions amongst themselves. If the Challenged player agrees to modify their action to the satisfaction of the Challenger, or successfully convinces the Challenger to drop the Challenge, then the Challenge ends without Bidding. (35)

Obstacle: A type of Complication in which the Originator sees (or inserts) some element in the scene that would make a declared Event difficult to accomplish. The Originator Buys Dice to represent that difficulty. The Winner of the Complication can then narrate how or if the Event plays out. (88, 90)

Originate a Complication: A Complication occurs in one of two ways: 1) when a player who Controls one Component is attempting to affect a Component Controlled by a different player or 2) when a player wishes to turn an Event described by another player into an Obstacle by Buying Dice for it. (88, 90)

Originator: The player who Originates a Complication is the Originator. They assemble a Source Dice Pool to oppose the Dice Pools built by Target Players. (91)

Ownership Trait: One Component can be marked as being a Possession of another Component with an Ownership Trait. The owned Component is automatically Introduced whenever the owner is Introduced. The owner's Importance is increased by the Importance of the Possession. The owner can be separated from the Possession by paying to Remove the Possession Trait (if such can be justified in the narrative). (67)

Pool: Shorthand for Dice Pool. (92)

Possession Trait: Any Trait representing an item that can be physically separated from its Component like a piece of equipment or gear. Separating the Possession costs 1 Coin and Creates the Possession as a new Component with an Ownership Trait linking it back to its original Component. (66)

Proper Name: Any Component can be given a Proper Name as a Trait. Like any Trait, it can be Drawn Upon for any Complication in which it applies. It is difficult to conceive of many situations where a mere name would apply to a Complication. However, there is a special rule for Characters (and rarely other Components). Because "named" Characters are always held to be more important than unnamed ones, a Character with a Proper Name can Draw Upon that name in any Complication in which they participate. (62)

Props: Any Component that is not a Location or a Character. Typically items, equipment, and gear, but also intangibles like religions or ideologies. (57)

Recorder: The player designated to maintain the log of Created Components, Scenes, and Events in the game. (12)

Refreshment: At the end of every scene and before the next one begins, all players receive a small number of additional Coins (typically 5) from the Bank added to their Wealth. (22)

Relationship Trait: Traits can depict family, professional, or emotional ties between Characters (or a Character and other Component). These Traits can be Drawn Upon any time the relationship applies. For definitional relationships, the same Coin buys a matching Relationship Trait for both related Components. (64)

Removing Traits: For 1 Coin, any one Trait of a Component can be crossed off of its record sheet. The rationale for this must be fully justified by the player causing the Removal (such as by damage or injury). (82)

Restoring Traits: For 1 Coin, any Trait that had been previously Removed can be Restored. The rationale for this must be fully justified by the player causing the Restoration (such as by healing or repair). (84)

Role: The first Trait that must be bought for any Component, the Role defines what that Component is or does for the story. This is often a position, or occupation for Characters, but can also be a story-based role. Roles can be Drawn Upon for any Complication in which they apply. (60)

Rules Gimmick: A formal means of proposing optional house rules during the game for 1 Coin. (19)

Scene: A game division in which the Framing Player Establishes a Location, Sets a Time, and Introduces Characters and Props. All players then take turns narrating events within the scene until the Framing Player ends it and a new scene is Framed. (22)

Social Contract: The Social Contract is an agreement between players about how a particular group intends to play. It can include rules on outside distractions, table talk, how loose the players will be with the rules, forbidden topics, pacing, and much more.

The Social Contract can be an informal understanding, a formal agreement, or elements can be proposed during play as individual Tenets. (17)

Source: Any Component whose Traits are going to be used to oppose the Targets in a Complication is a Source of the Complication. (90, 92)

Source Player: The player who Controls a Source Component or Buys Dice as an Obstacle is a Source Player and will have the opportunity to build a Source Dice Pool. The Originator of a Complication will always build a Source Dice Pool. (90, 92)

Story Element: A Story Element is a Tenet which defines the type of story about to be told and includes items like genre, theme, setting, mood, and situations. These make up the "type" of story the players want to tell. (15)

Sub Component: A Component can be made a Sub Component of a Master Component by buying a Trait indicating the connection (often the Role will indicate this connection). The Sub Component has access to all of the Traits of the Master Component and each Sub Component is free to Draw Upon them during Complications. The Sub Component's Importance is determined only by its own Traits, not including those inherited from the Master. (70)

Successes: When the Dice Pools in a Complication are rolled, each die that comes up a 1-5 is a Success. The side with the most Successes is the Winning Side, the other side is the Losing Side. (105)

Take Over: For 1 Coin, you can take Control over any Component in a scene currently Controlled by another player. It does not have to be your turn to do this, nor does the Take Over make it your turn. Complications or Dialog are often the result of a Take Over. Alternatively, Take Overs can allow you to avoid Complications by giving you control of both sides of the conflict. (51)

Target: Any Component that is going to be affected as the result of a Complication is a Target. (91)

Target Player: The player who Controls a Target Component is a Target Player and will have the opportunity to build a Target Dice Pool. (91)

Tenets: Tenets are rules of the game. They can be Social Contract Issues, Story Elements, or Rules Gimmicks. They define how and what a group intends to play. Tenets cost 1 Coin and only one can be proposed on a player's turn. (13)

Traits: Traits are like adjectives that describe Components. The more Traits a Component has, the more Important it is. Traits can also be Drawn Upon to provide dice during Complications. Traits cost 1 Coin. (57)

Wealth: A player's supply of Coins is called his Wealth. Players begin with a supply of Coins at the beginning of each game (typically 25), and this is replenished through Complications and Refreshment. (11)

Winning Side: The side rolling more Successes in a Complication. Each player on the Winning Side gets a number of Bonus Coins equal to the sum on all Successful dice in their Pool to narrate the outcome of the Complication. All players on the Winning Side get to narrate before any players on the Losing Side. (105)

UNIVERSALIS
REFERENCE

ACTIONS YOU CAN DO ANY TIME

- ○ Spend a Coin to Interrupt and begin your own turn.
- ○ Spend a Coin to Interrupt and Originate a Complication.
- ○ Take Over a Component in the scene for 1 Coin.
- ○ Initiate a Challenge. Bid Coins if necessary.
- ○ Engage in dialog for a character you Control.

ACTIONS YOU CAN DO ONLY ON YOUR TURN

1) Scene Narration Activity (Chapter 4)
   - ○ Establish or change the scene's location to a new or existing location for 1 Coin.
   - ○ Introduce an existing Component into the scene for 1 Coin.
   - ○ Exit a Component from a scene for 1 Coin.
   - ○ Describe an Event for 1 Coin.

2) World Building Activity (Chapter 5)
   - ○ Create a new Component and Introduce it into the scene or not for 1 Coin.
   - ○ Add, Remove, or Restore a Trait for 1 Coin per Trait.
   - ○ Reduce or Restore Importance for 1 Coin per Level.

3) Game Tenet Activity (Chapter 2)
   - ○ Propose a new (or modify an existing) Social Contract issue for 1 Coin.
   - ○ Propose a new (or modify an existing) Story Element for 1 Coin.
   - ○ Propose a new (or modify an existing) Rules Gimmick for 1 Coin.

4) Complication Activity (Chapter 6)
   - ○ Originate a Complication with one or more Components you do not Control.
   - ○ Draw Upon a Trait to add dice to a Complication Dice Pool
   - ○ Buy Dice (and justify the purchase) for a Complication Dice Pool for 1 Coin apiece.
   - ○ Roll the dice, determine the winner, and spend or keep Bonus Coins.

CAPES

A SUPERHERO GAME WITH HEART!

In our hearts, we want our heroes to be like us, and to share our important strengths and weaknesses. Yes, they should be better, stronger, braver. They should be invulnerable to bullets, stronger than continental drift, fast enough to escape an exploding star. But they must not be invulnerable to heart-ache, stronger than love, or fast enough to escape their own past.

http://www.museoffire.com/Games/

YOU CAN SAVE THE WORLD, BUT ARE YOU WILLING TO PAY THE PRICE?

A hero is more than a costume, a battlecry,
and powers beyond those of mortal men.

Superheroes triumph
over heart-rending tragedy,
rising—despite unyielding burdens—to face
the challenges that threaten the world.

DO YOU HAVE WHAT IT TAKES TO STAND BACK UP?

"... a perfect Silver Age story arc
right out of Stan Lee's playbook."

—Ken Hite, Out of the Box

A role-playing game of superheroic melodrama
from Incarnadine Press

incarnadine.indie-rpgs.com

POLARIS

Chivalric Tragedy at the Utmost North

Image by Boris Artzybasheff

A game by Ben Lehman

Available now

http://www.tao-games.com

TAO GAMES